PAUL

PAUL

In Fresh Perspective

N. T. WRIGHT

Fortress Press
Minneapolis

PAUL
In Fresh Perspective

First Fortress Press paperback edition 2009

This volume is published in collaboration with SPCK, London.

Cover design: Laurie Ingram
Cover image: St. Paul, fourteenth-century mosaic from the Kariye Camii, Istanbul. © Sonia Holliday Photography.

ISBN 978-0-8006-6357-5

The paper used in this publication meets the minimum requirements of American National Standard for Information Sciences — Permanence of Paper for Printed Library Materials, ANSI Z329.48-1984.

Manufactured in the U.S.A.

for Charlie Moule

Contents

Part II
STRUCTURES

monograph *The Climax of the Covenant* (T. & T. Clark, 1992) and the Commentary on Romans in the *New Interpreters Bible* vol. X (Abingdon, 2003).[1] I hope that these further explorations will stimulate fresh thought, study and above all delight in one of the most powerful and seminal minds of the first or any century.

The latter claim is not exaggerated. Despite the long-standing English tendency to sneer at Paul and to press him for answers to questions he didn't ask, I persist in regarding him as the intellectual equal of Plato, Aristotle or Seneca, even though the demands of his overall vocation, coupled with his dense style, mean that what we possess of his thought is compressed into a fraction of their written compass. Whichever angle you come at him from, there will be surprises and riches in store; again and again, just when you think you've got his measure, he chuckles and forces you to read a passage you thought you knew well in a quite different light, and then, if you dare, to attempt what he had already accomplished, that is, to reflect on how the different viewpoints integrate one with another. Reflecting on that task makes me feel somewhat like a middle-aged man in Wellington boots trying to imitate a quicksilver-footed ballet dancer; but if my lumbering around after Paul reveals all too clearly how far I still have to go in following him exactly, I hope it will at least stimulate those with fresher minds and more youthful energy to do better, perhaps by sparking off some ideas with those in particular who are at an early stage in their careers and have the opportunity to study Paul intensively for themselves and come up with challenges, modifications and fresh proposals of their own. I have to say that for me there has been no more stimulating exercise, for the mind, the heart, the imagination and the spirit, than trying to think Paul's thoughts after him and constantly to be stirred up to fresh glimpses of God's ways and purposes with the world and with us strange human creatures. The church and the academy both urgently need a new generation of teachers and preachers who will give themselves totally to the delighted study of the text and allow themselves to be taken wherever it leads, to think new thoughts arising out of the text and to dare to try them out in word and deed. I trust that these lectures, and now this book, will serve as a reminder that studying the New Testament remains not only the core of a good theology degree, but one of the premier intellectual and personal challenges available in any academy; and that studying Paul in particular constitutes one of the most demanding and rewarding of sub-disciplines.

Let me then outline the argument of this book. The first chapter forms a general introduction, after which the next three chapters look at major Pauline themes which have been highlighted in some recent study, and which allow us to put down some preliminary markers about the way Paul's mind worked. Then the fifth, sixth and seventh chapters form a miniature systematic account of the main theological contours of Paul's thought. A final chapter looks more briefly at some key themes which our study may place in a new light.

In each case what I am doing is not so much presenting several discrete and separate aspects of Paul's life and thought, but rather taking a different path up the same large and craggy mountain. Reading Paul is in fact a bit like climbing a mountain; there are many routes up Scafell Pike or Ben Nevis, and those who are used only to the easy tourist path sometimes forget that scaling the vertical crags is not only more exciting but might sometimes get you to the top more quickly. What I am trying to do is to map various paths, each of which, I believe, leads to the summit. Like the great Alfred Wainwright in the English Lake District, I am trying to provide a kind of sketch-book for those who want to attempt the routes for themselves.

In allowing something of the format, and even the occasional colloquial style, of the original lectures to remain, I am conscious that every paragraph could attract footnotes to itself like wasps round a jar of honey, and that this would make the book quite a different sort of thing. I intend it rather to stand as a pointer to the fuller treatment which is supposed to form volume IV of my series 'Christian Origins and the Question of God', where at least the key issues may be treated in more detail. Nor is there any question of engaging in detailed debate with the many writers who have addressed similar topics, tempting though it will be to set some records straight and perhaps even settle some old scores. Those who want to follow up particular topics and themes will find the leads they require in the other works I have already referred to. I will, however, refer occasionally to works which I have found helpful, and provide a slightly fuller list in the bibliography.

My wife and I were fortunate indeed to be looked after in Cambridge by several friends while the lectures were being given.

Professor Graham Stanton, the Lady Margaret Professor of Divinity, was our host at the Faculty, and he and his colleagues made sure we were cared for in true Cambridge style. Dr Barry Everitt, the Master of Downing College, and his wife Jane, and Lord Wilson of Tillyorn, the Master of Peterhouse, and Lady Wilson, provided splendid hospitality and quiet space in which I was able to pull my notes together into a set of coherent discourses. Some of the lectures were given in slightly different format as the Hoon-Bullock Lectures at First Presbyterian Church, San Antonio, Texas in November 2004; some others, similarly adjusted, at the Auburn Avenue Presbyterian Church Annual Pastors' Conference in Monroe, Louisiana, in January 2005; others again, lightly reworked, as the Annual Theological Lectures at Queen's University, Belfast, and as the Firth Lectures in Nottingham University, in February and March 2005 respectively. Once again my wife and I are deeply grateful for the kind care and lavish hospitality of our hosts in both locations.

The dedication reflects an old debt, both academic and personal. From my earliest days as a student of the New Testament the name of C. F. D. Moule was one to be spoken with awe, and his works read with enthusiasm. I was then enormously fortunate to live in Cambridge when he was in the early days of 'retirement' there, and to enjoy his friendship and encouragement. He then became, after the sad early death of my own teacher George Caird, a kind of adopted mentor, and has to this day continued to read what I write and to make shrewd, kindly and always telling comments upon it. Now that I live in the house which his great-uncle, Bishop H. C. G. Moule, occupied with distinction a hundred years ago, I find myself giving thanks for the Moule family and its heritage at several levels. This small book, with its Cambridge and Durham connections, seems an appropriate way of bringing this gratitude into public expression.

N. T. Wright
Auckland Castle

Part I
THEMES

1

Paul's World, Paul's Legacy

1. The Three Worlds of Paul

I spoke in the Preface of studying Paul being like finding different ways up a mountain. By shifting this metaphor only a little, I arrive at an initial observation which gets us into Paul's world, the first main subject of this introductory chapter. Actually, we might equally be speaking of worlds, plural; part of the excitement of reading Paul is the fact that he straddled at least three worlds, so that whatever he says demands to be heard within three different acoustic chambers, which may or may not have been audible to one another even though Paul intended them to resonate simultaneously.

Reverting to the mountain metaphor, I envisage Paul in terms of a hill I used to climb as a boy in the north-west Pennines, where having climbed up from the Yorkshire side you could stand, with your right foot still in Yorkshire, your left foot in Lancashire, and, stretching forwards, touching the ancient and much-mourned county of Westmorland. In the same way, Paul lived in (at least) three worlds. Only if we bear each of them in mind will we have any chance of understanding the contours of his writing.

The first world, the one by which he ascended the mountain, was of course Judaism. Second-Temple Judaism has been studied more in the last generation than in the previous millennium, and new research continues to pour out on Scrolls, Pharisees, early rabbis, and so on, not to mention the relevant archaeological discoveries. Yet a broadly coherent picture can and does emerge from the confusing mass of information, just as the climber can pick out the main rivers and roads without necessarily being able to see how every lane and stream join up. Second-Temple Judaism was a many-sided and vibrant mixture of what we would now call (though they would not have recognized these distinctions) religion, faith, culture and politics. But even its clashing elements were usually clashing about the same issues: what it meant to be part of God's people, to be loyal to Torah, to maintain Jewish identity in the face of the all-encroaching pagan world, and (above all in the view of some) to await the coming of God's kingdom, of the 'age to come' promised by the prophets, of Israel's redemption, hoping that when that day dawned one might have a share in the coming vindication and blessing. This was the world from which Paul came, and in which he remained even though he said things which nobody within that world had thought of saying before and which many in that world found shocking, even destructive. Imagine how a suspicious Yorkshireman might wonder if our climber was secretly swapping his white rose for a red one.

The second world was that of the Greek, or Hellenistic, culture which by Paul's day had permeated most of the recesses of the Eastern Mediterranean world and a good deal beyond. Ever since Alexander the Great three hundred and more years earlier, Greek had become not only everybody's second language, like English today, but in many parts everybody's assumed framework of thought. Again, there are of course many varieties of first-century Hellenism, but the culture and philosophy, and not least, when we think of Paul, the rhetorical style of the Greek world was powerful and pervasive. You only have to read a few pages of Paul's younger contemporary Epictetus to sense that, though they would have disagreed radically in several beliefs, they shared a common language and style of arguing. At points you might almost think they lived on the same street. Paul is at home, in fact, in the street-level world of Hellenistic discourse, while being aware of the need, as he puts it, to 'take every thought captive to obey the Messiah'.[1] He makes fruitful use of the language and imagery of the pagan moralists while constantly infusing it with fresh content. Nor is this simply a matter of accommodating to another culture, of playing at both ends of the field at once. Precisely because his Jewish tradition taught him that the one God of Abraham was the creator of the whole earth and that all human beings were made in his image, he, like some of his contemporaries such as the author of the Wisdom of Solomon, was able to mark out a firm platform within Jewish thought itself from which to address the inhabitants, and indeed the rulers, of the rest of the world.

And it was the world rulers of Paul's day, and the world which they were bent on creating, that formed the third sphere which Paul inhabited, corresponding in my illustration to the third county which our climber, with both feet firmly planted, could reach forwards and touch. Paul, to the surprise of some both then and now, was a Roman citizen, and if we take even a moderate view of the historicity of Acts he seems to have made good occasional use of the privilege. But, as with his Jewish and his Hellenistic worlds, he was not an uncritical inhabitant of Caesar's large domain. His positioning of himself vis-à-vis the Roman empire, with its ideology and burgeoning emperor-cult, is a theme much discussed today, and I shall devote the entire fourth chapter to it.

In forming the third point in our triangle of Paul's world, the Roman context integrates closely with the other two. Judaism had a tradition of critique of pagan empire stretching back nearly a millennium, with Egypt and the Exodus as its ultimate backdrop. It was not hard for a first-century Jew to retell the old stories of oppression and liberation and envisage a new actor playing the lead villain. The first time I attended a Purim celebration, in West Jerusalem in 1989, my Jewish hosts were embarrassed at how obvious it was, as the story of the book of Esther unfolded, to see who, in the minds of many in the room, was being cast as the present-day equivalent of Haman and his sons. Powerful stories suggest their own recapitulative hermeneutics. And when Paul believed that Israel's God had at last sent his Messiah to be the world's rightful Lord, the clash of worlds, the rebirth of images, became inevitable, generating new theological as well as political questions and possibilities. Paul remained firmly within the Jewish tradition in his response to the claims of Rome.

At the same time, Roman imperial ideology and cult drew substantially on the Hellenistic world for its philosophical and ideological underpinnings. We should never forget that most of the Roman world, and a fair slice of the capital city itself, spoke Greek as its first and sometimes its only language. Paul lived, worked, thought and wrote within a complex and multiply integrated world. Though his phrase 'all things to all people' often now seems merely to indicate someone prepared to trim their sails to every passing wind, Paul meant it in a more robust sense. He had been entrusted with a Jewish message for the whole world, and part of the way in which the message was to get out was by his embodying in himself (in ways that caused some then, and cause some still, to raise an eyebrow) the outreach of Israel's one true God to the wider world of the Gentiles. Paul remained a firm monotheist, and as we shall see he explored and exploited that belief to the full.

But it was a disturbingly redefined monotheism. To the three worlds which together form Paul's context we must add a fourth, already in being by the time of his conversion, a world which formed, we may suppose, an almost equally disturbing setting. He belonged to the family of the Messiah, to the people of God he referred to as the *ekklēsia*, the 'called-out ones', corresponding in some ways (though not others) both to the Jewish synagogue community and to civic gatherings in the Gentile world. A good deal of his effort was devoted to arguing, from one direction and another, that though this people was the true family of Abraham, though it brought together people who lived ordinary lives in the wider pagan world, and though it made its way within Caesar's empire, it was in fact a different *sort* of thing from any of these. It was defined neither by ethnic origin nor by social class; it was neither a club, nor a cult, nor a guild, though onlookers must often have thought it was one of these. The church, the assembly of Jesus the Messiah, formed (in Paul's view) a world of its own, standing in a unique relation to the other three worlds, and deriving from them, in various overlapping ways, the sundry dynamics which caused Paul so many problems. But more of that anon. For Paul, to be 'in the Messiah', to belong to the Messiah's body, meant embracing an identity rooted in Judaism, lived out in the Hellenistic world, and placing a counter-claim against Caesar's aspiration to world domination, while being both more and less than a simple combination of elements from within those three. Paul would have insisted that there was something unique about this fourth world, and he would have traced that uniqueness back to the person of Jesus himself and to his incorporative role as Messiah.

Thus far, the world of Paul. As should be apparent, this world could profitably be described in terms of its multiple overlapping and sometimes competing *narratives*: the story of God and Israel from the Jewish side; the pagan stories about their gods and the world, and the implicit narratives around which individual pagans constructed their identities, from the Greco-Roman sides; and particularly the great narratives of empire, both the large-scale ones we find in Virgil and Livy and elsewhere and the smaller, implicit ones of local culture. Likewise, this world could be described in terms of its *symbols*: within Judaism, Temple, Torah, Land and family identity; within paganism, the multiple symbols of nation, kingship, religion and culture; in Rome in particular, the symbols (from coins to arches to temples to military might) which spoke of the single great world empire. We could add to this the characteristic *praxis* of the different overlapping cultures, both the ways of living which expressed and embodied personal aspiration as well as mere survival, and the ways which were adopted as a result of particular social or ethical teaching. And we could also plot the kind of answers we could expect, within the different cultures, to the great *questions* which lie behind every worldview: who are we, where are we, what's wrong, what's the solution, and what time is it? I have outlined elsewhere this four-part analysis of worldviews (story, symbol, praxis and question), and though there is no space in these lectures to elaborate it explicitly in relation to Paul it is important to keep it in mind as a framework to which we shall refer from time to time.[2]

I want to say a little more at this stage about the first of these levels in particular. A good deal of attention has recently been given to the narrative dimensions of Paul's thought, and I regard this as one of the key elements in what has come to be known as the 'new perspective' on Paul, about which I shall say more presently.[3] The present interest can be traced back not least to the doctoral dissertation of Richard B. Hays. Hays studied the implicit storyline condensed within some extremely dense fragments of Galatians, and argued that Paul was working with, and summarizing, a much larger narrative in which the death and resurrection of Jesus (and in particular his 'faithfulness') played the decisive role.[4] But once the narrative genie has been let out of the bottle, not least in a world with its eyes newly opened by contemporary literary study, you can't get it back in; and now all kinds of aspects of Paul are being tested for implicit and explicit storylines. Despite the wishes and efforts of some, this cannot be dismissed either as the superimposition on Paul of alien ideas or as a mere post-liberal fad. It certainly does not reduce Paul's thought, as some have darkly hinted, to a world of 'story' *over against* 'doctrine' on the one hand or real life on the other. To take an obvious example, Jewish literature from the Bible to the present day is soaked in certain controlling stories, such as those of Abraham, of the Exodus, and of exile and return, so that a small allusion to one of these within a Jewish source is usually a safe indication that we should understand the whole narrative to be at least hovering in the background. When we find allusions to the same stories in Paul we are not merely invited but obliged to follow them up and lay bare the narrative world he would have taken for granted. Within second-Temple Judaism, we must resist the cautious minimalism that threatens here as elsewhere to reduce scholarship to embattled silence. There is no point standing shivering on the one sandbank that the tide of narrative has not covered. The only way to safety, however paradoxical, is to dive in and swim.

The turn to narrative is, in fact, one of the most significant developments which the 'new perspective' revolution has precipitated, going far beyond anything Sanders himself said or (I believe) thought.[5] I want to insist that this be seen both as part of the developing 'new perspective' and as a central, not merely illustrative or peripheral, element in Paul. But, equally, it is important to stress that it is also a matter of sheer *history*: understanding how stories worked in the ancient world, and how a small allusion could and did summon up an entire implicit narrative, including narratives within which speaker and hearer believed themselves to be living, is a vital tool. I have in mind here the remarkable new book on Nero by the Princeton professor Edward Champlin, in which he demonstrates in great detail, in parallel with the work of Zanker and others, the way in which the rich and varied mythologies of ancient Greece and Rome functioned in the minds and imaginations of ordinary people, so that even a small allusion to Aeneas, to Agamemnon or Orestes, to Oedipus and other characters, would at once present to an audience – for instance, when Nero took the stage in carefully chosen roles – an entire storyline which we have to reconstruct with difficulty, step by step, but which ordinary people in that world knew without difficulty. As Champlin says, 'So common was the vocabulary of myth in daily life, high and low, that it was one of the hardest currencies in public debate: it provided simple, universal codes which everyone could comprehend.'[6] How this worked out in Nero's own specific career, and the claims he made, is relevant to the study of early Christianity in a number of ways, not least of course to the book of

Revelation. But for our present purposes I want to insist that the implicit narratives which Paul evokes, both in obvious passages like Romans 4 and Galatians 3, where the entire narrative of Abraham as the father of the true people of God is clearly in view (though you would never know this from some of the recent critics of the 'new perspective', any more than from Sanders himself), and in far less obvious passages like the quotation from Psalm 116 (LXX 115) in 2 Corinthians 4.13 – these implicit narratives were clear to Paul and would have been clear to his readers. Even small turns of phrase can carry massive implications. I remember listening to a politician speaking about police work, and referring from time to time to 'the north of Ireland', and realizing that he had strong reasons for not saying 'Northern Ireland', let alone 'Ulster'.

It is not simply that Paul alludes to a number of well-known narratives. Some critics of narrative readings of Paul have reacted as though this is just embroidery around the central theological points, which are taken to be non-narratival. I want to insist that Paul's whole point is precisely that with the coming, the death and the resurrection of Jesus the Messiah a new chapter has opened within the story in which he had believed himself to be living, and that understanding what that story is and how this chapter is indeed a radically new moment within it provides one of the central clues to everything else he says, not least the questions of justification and the law upon which the 'perspective'-battles have been so often fought out. Refusing to admit narrative into this debate is therefore like refusing to put petrol in a car because you know that what you need to drive is tyres and a steering wheel.

Of course, we will go on debating what precisely that controlling narrative was, and how Paul understood it. But as I and others have shown, the great stories of Abraham, of Exodus, of David (this one meets particular resistance, of course), and of exile and restoration (this one, even more so) create not merely a rich narrative backcloth from which motifs can be drawn at will to produce a resonant typology but also, much more so, a single narrative line, containing typological recapitulations but not reducible to them, in which Paul believed that he and his contemporaries were living. Like Livy telling the story of Rome's former greatness in order to lead the eye up to the new world of Augustus; and, even more so, like Qumran telling the story of Israel's prophecies in order to claim that the promises were now being fulfilled in their own community, promises precisely of return from exile; like 4 Ezra re-reading Daniel, parallel to the hints we find in Josephus, in order to claim that the long apocalyptic drama was now reaching its point of denouement, so Paul invokes the great stories of God, Israel and the world because his view of salvation itself, and with it justification and all the rest, is not an ahistorical scheme about how individuals come into a right relationship with God, but rather tells how the God of Abraham has fulfilled his promises at last through the apocalyptic death and resurrection of his own beloved Son. As we shall see in Chapter 3, what some call 'apocalyptic', properly understood within its first-century framework, does indeed lie at the heart of Paul's theology, not cutting against the continuity, the promise-fulfilling character, of Paul's covenantal theology, but rather completing it and filling it out, preventing it from collapsing, as both Reformed theology and some versions of the 'new perspective' do, into being so positive about continuity as to leave no room for the Pauline emphasis on the cross of the Messiah, and for the consequent critique of all human pride and system.

The narrative turn in Pauline exegesis is thus, in my view, one of the most significant developments within the world opened up by the 'new perspective'. It belongs closely with that reading of Paul's use of the Old Testament, opened up once more by Richard Hays and others, in which (as in so many Jewish texts, and as Champlin has pointed out in many non-Jewish ones) a single small allusion can conjure up an entire world of thought. This is one of the points, of course, at which this 'new perspective' development goes completely against Sanders' own exegetical proposals. Notoriously, he suggested that Paul quoted the Old Testament more or less at random, without regard for context, so that, for instance, he simply ran through a mental concordance in search of some scriptural proof for his theology of justification by faith, and came up with the two passages in which 'righteousness' and 'faith' were combined, namely Genesis 15 and Habakkuk 2. It is hard to argue against such determination not to see what is in fact there in the texts. Often the ultimate argument for a piece of exegesis is simply to read the passage with this set of spectacles on and see if it does not come up in three dimensions, over against the flat and fuzzy reading you get without them. We need, at points like this, to be more aware than we sometimes are of the implicit hypothesis-and-verification structure of our various debates.

Paying attention to the underlying narrative structure of Paul's thought, then, is not simply a matter of recognizing the implicit narratives in Paul and drawing out their implications for detailed exegesis. Something much deeper, more revolutionary, is going on when we start to unearth these implicit stories, and I suspect it is resistance to this element that is currently driving both the resistance to recognizing narratives at all and, more particularly, the increasingly forceful resistance to the so-called 'new perspective'. The main point about narratives in the second-Temple Jewish world, and in that of Paul, is not simply that people liked telling stories as illustrations of, or scriptural proofs for, this or that experience or doctrine, but rather that second-Temple Jews believed themselves to be *actors within* a real-life narrative. To put it another way, they were not merely storytellers who used their folklore (in their case, mostly the Bible) to illustrate the otherwise unrelated joys and sorrows, trials and triumphs, of everyday life. Their narratives could and did function typologically, that is, by providing a pattern which could be laid as a template across incidents and stories from another period without any historical continuity to link the two together. But the main function of their stories was to remind them of earlier and (they hoped) characteristic moments *within the single, larger story* which stretched from the creation of the world and the call of Abraham right forwards to their own day, and (they hoped) into the future. If I can risk two absurdly different analogies, they were in the position not so much of a lonely young girl reading *Jane Eyre* and dreaming of possible parallels, as of a cricketer, about to go out and bat in a match whose long story, and earlier episodes, has left the game nicely poised and ready for fresh action which will bring the story forwards to its conclusion. One could without difficulty demonstrate, for instance, that different readings of Romans 4 can be measured in terms of the way the story of Abraham is deemed to function: is it a mere scriptural proof of justification by faith, or what? As I shall argue in the next chapter, Paul has the entire story of Genesis 15 in mind, and reveals in the last few verses that the story which began at that point has now reached its decisive, and potentially match-winning, stage. We could also note the way in which the events of AD 70 and 135 had the effect precisely of bringing to a full and grinding stop the implicit narrative which second-Temple Jews had been living in, thereby generating a new form of normative Judaism which would find its primary expression in terms not of story but of dehistoricized law-exposition. But in Paul's day the story was in full swing. He and many of his Jewish contemporaries were eager to discover where precisely the plot had got to and what role they were called to play within it.

This in turn is grounded – and I believe this to be a vital underlying principle of all Paul's thought – on the belief that the one true God is the creator, the ruler and the coming judge of the whole world. Monotheism of the Jewish style (creation, providence, final justice), which Paul re-emphasizes as he refashions it, generates just this sense of underlying narrative, the historical and as yet unfinished story of creation and covenant, to which the individual stories such as those of Abraham and the Exodus contribute, and whose flavour they reinforce, but which goes beyond mere typology into strong historical continuity. This was, after all, the point of much of the exilic and post-exilic literature. God did not abandon his people when he packed them off to Babylon. Much of the second-Temple literature is precisely concerned to tell the story again and again to show how the plot was progressing and, perhaps, reaching its climax. Unless we recognize this and factor it into our thinking about Paul and his Jewish world from the very start we will have no chance of grasping the fundamental structures of his thought. And if, as has so often been done, we substitute for his controlling narratives those of other traditions and cultures, we are asking for hermeneutical trouble.

It is this element, I suggest, which enables us both to re-articulate the 'new perspective' and to ward off the by now standard criticisms of it. This is somewhat ironic, in that neither E. P. Sanders nor James Dunn, the two leading proponents of the so-called 'new perspective', have developed to any extent the narrative understanding of Paul which Hays and others, including myself, have proposed. More of this anon; particularly in the second chapter, when I shall be looking at creation and covenant as major themes, indeed as an integrated major theme, of Pauline thought, and arguing for a particular view of salvation not as an *a*historical rescue *from* the world but as the *trans*historical redemption *of* the world. This is the point at which the single narrative, which began with creation and moves forward through covenant, reaches, at some point in the future from both Paul's perspective and our own, its appropriate fulfilment. What matters in narrative readings of Paul, I suggest, is not so much whether or not implicit narratives are to be found within his writings (that can hardly be denied), but what *kind* of narrative we are dealing with, and what role it plays both in Judaism and in Paul. In fact, we could even propose that the kind of narrative varies in direct relation to the putative content; but this, too, I must leave for another occasion.

The fulfilment of the covenant, resulting in new covenant and new creation, is accomplished, for Paul, by the particular events of Jesus' death and resurrection. I shall argue in the third chapter that Paul understood those events both messianically (reading *Christos* in Paul as normally meaning 'Messiah') and apocalyptically. This then points forward, as we might expect within both messianic Judaism and apocalyptic Judaism, to the confrontation between the gospel of Jesus and the gospel of Caesar; this will be the theme of the fourth chapter. The second, third and fourth chapters will all thus explore central themes within the controlling implicit story, or at least one of the controlling implicit stories, of second-Temple Judaism, and show how Paul both modified them and made them his own. This was at the heart of his work as he, driven by the gospel of Jesus and (he would have added) the power of the Spirit, announced the Jewish Messiah in the world where Greece had taught people to think and Rome had compelled them to fearful submission.

2. Fighting over Paul's Legacy: Perspectives Old, New and Different

The question of Paul's legacy is in principle much more complicated than that of his world, but most of those complexities are beyond the reach both of this book and of my competence. Like too many New Testament scholars, I am largely ignorant of the Pauline exegesis of all but a few of the fathers and reformers. The Middle Ages, and the seventeenth and eighteenth centuries, had plenty to say about Paul, but I have not read it. Similarly, we are in danger today of being drawn in to the scholarly version of our modern imperial world, as the focus of scholarship has shifted from Germany, which was still making the running when I began doctoral work thirty years ago, to the USA. This is potentially very misleading, since there is plenty of work still being done in Europe, not to mention a whole range of scholarship emerging from the Third World, not least Africa. The experience of the earlier German scholarship which, as hindsight enables us to see clearly, was inevitably driven by the pressing concerns of the Weimar Republic, the Nazi period and then the post-war reconstruction, should warn us against hitching our wagons to the scholarship, and hence the powerful implicit questions and narratives, of any particular contemporary culture to the exclusion of others, especially when the culture in question happens to be in a position of unchallenged power. But we cannot stand in more than one place at once, and while recognizing and deploring the partial nature of our vision we have to do our best, trusting in Kipling's nice phrase that there is a time to paint The Thing As We See It for The God of Things As They Are.[7]

And the 'thing as I see it' is of course powerfully conditioned, as is all contemporary western scholarship, by the discussions of Paul that have taken place in Europe and North America over the last two hundred years. We postmoderns may chafe in our slavery to the Enlightenment, but the way to freedom is to challenge the slave-master. Moses had to do business with Pharaoh, not with the ruler of some other country. And from within the Enlightenment the major themes of discussion of Paul have been, obviously, fourfold: history, theology, exegesis and contemporary relevance.

These have frequently been confused with one another, but they are essentially separable. It is one thing to locate Paul historically and to attempt to understand his social and cultural location, the pattern of his religion (both his own experience and that which he sought to inculcate), and its links to other movements of his day. It is a different thing, though of course overlapping, to attempt to describe the patterns of his worldview and theology, to plot what he said about God and the world, about evil and its solution, about what it meant to be human and how one might be more fully or truly human – these are the perennial theological questions in any tradition, though surprisingly most people today are unaware of the fact – and to note how his specific historical challenges drew forth from him varied but again interlocking expressions of this theology. History and theology, not least within any worldview that draws strongly on Judaism, are bound to impact on one another, but they are not the same thing. Both disciplines draw on, and in turn feed back into, the third very different sphere of activity, that of exegesis itself, which I regard as both the starting point and the finishing point of the task.

History, theology and exegesis are always done – not only sometimes, and not only by preachers – with at least half an eye on the results that may be expected in the scholar's own world. Those who regard Paul as a pestilent, self-contradictory, rambling neurotic are just as eager that their hearers should see him this way too (so that, for instance, they might then the more cheerfully reject Paul's ethical teaching) as are those who regard his every word as proceeding directly from the mouth of God. Neutrality is impossible. Heisenberg's uncertainty principle, according to which the act of observing something changes the thing being observed, making accurate reporting impossible by definition, has worked its way through into postmodern critical theory and has thereby come at last with a little pin to bore through the castle walls of imperial objectivism. As I have argued elsewhere, the only way forward from this point is by means of a robust critical realism, generating both a historical and a theological epistemology far removed both from the revived positivism on offer in some quarters and the enthusiastic subjectivism advanced elsewhere, and dependent for its effectiveness on the power, once more, of the stories it tells.

The non-neutrality of Pauline scholarship on all sides is easy to name across the twentieth century. It was no accident that Albert Schweitzer read early Christianity in the light of Jewish apocalyptic, or at least a Nietzschean understanding thereof. It was no accident that Rudolf Bultmann took up Heideggerian existentialism at the time he did, or that he read Paul in this light. It was no accident that W. D. Davies wrote his sea-change book *Paul and Rabbinic Judaism* at the very moment when news was coming in of the Nazi Holocaust, when Europe was turning away from the neo-paganism which had generated such a thing and asking whether its negative assessment of Judaism had been a ghastly mistake. It was no accident, within that world, both that the Swedish Lutheran Krister Stendahl should challenge the prevailing German Lutheran tradition in his famous essay on 'Paul and the Introspective Conscience of the West', and that Ernst Käsemann should defend it with the warning that to substitute salvation-history for justification was to follow the route taken by the German Christians who had supported Hitler. The implicit moral watershed of the twentieth century (analyse the ideas which sustained Hitler, and shun even their fleeting appearance) was evoked then, as it has continued to be whenever Paul and Judaism are discussed. The same debate continues to inform Pauline scholarship, for instance in J. Louis Martyn's staunch support for what some call 'apocalyptic' over against what some call 'covenant'; and you only have to mention the word 'supersessionism' to evoke the chimneys of Auschwitz. It was no accident that, in the USA in the 1970s, E. P. Sanders should (a) discuss Judaism and Paul in terms of 'patterns of religion', (b) defend Judaism against the charge that it had one particular pattern of religion, and (c) propose that Paul and Judaism were not after all so far apart, and that Paul's distance from Judaism came simply as a result of his personal experience rather than sustained theological reasoning from first principles. It was no accident that this view should have taken off like a rocket in America and many parts of Britain, and spluttered like a damp squib in Germany; nor that others in America should then pass laws forbidding all contemporary fireworks and restricting entertainment to old movies of exegetical pyrotechnics from the sixteenth century. Neo-Puritanism is itself, of course, a thoroughly inculturated phenomenon.

Nor are the current waves of enthusiasm free from contextual and cultural agendas. It is no accident that Richard Hays pioneered both the narrative approach to Paul and a fresh way of understanding his use of the Old Testament after years of inhaling the postliberal and canonical air of New Haven. It is no accident that Troels Engberg-Pedersen in Copenhagen has energetically proposed fresh readings of Paul which owe little to traditional Jewish or Christian ideas and much to first-century pagan philosophy. It is certainly no accident that Richard Horsley has pioneered the new political readings of Paul from a below-the-tracks university in Boston where it is taken for granted that today's monolithic American empire is, if not the source of all evil, at least one of its major current conduits; and, once more, it is no accident that some are trying to dismiss this new emphasis as a mere leftie fad. And, finally, it is no accident that the vast majority of Christians in the world today read Paul with blissful ignorance of all these movements and counter-movements.

Are they therefore any better off? By no means. Only if we start with the assumption that what we ought to have is pure, unsullied objectivism will we conclude that this string of non-accidents reduces previous scholarship to a worthless pile of words. The fact that there are all kinds of non-accidents waiting to happen among the readers of this book (if I dare put it like that) does not mean that they will be without value. I am neither a determinist nor a nihilist. The fact that we can locate all these movements of thought meaningfully within the culture of the last hundred years could even be taken as an indication that a beneficent Providence was so ordering the affairs of the world that fresh light would constantly be shed on scripture, though that would run the risk of a different sort of determinism.

I would prefer to insist on three things. First, there are such things as texts; however much we deconstruct them, they bounce back with renewed challenge, and Paul's texts have a particularly strong track record in this respect. Second, there are such things as fresh and compelling readings of texts; new pairs of eyes, no doubt with new motives but none the worse for that, scan familiar words and hear unfamiliar messages, and then – this bit is enormously important – test them out, not merely on those who share the reader's cultural and religious predispositions but on those who do not. The public nature of scholarship is part of the surge towards insight, despite the danger of mere collusion, of a ghetto masquerading as the world. And, third, I do believe in the mysterious, unpredictable and usually hidden work of the Holy Spirit. It would be odd to omit this from a discussion of Paul of all people; rather as though one were to discuss Beethoven's sonatas while dismissing from one's mind the possibility that there might actually be such a thing as a piano. Even if one cannot play the piano oneself, one should normally reckon that someone who could do so would have a head start, not a handicap, in discussing the music.

The fact, therefore, that we all live within contexts and that some ideas are more thinkable in some places and periods than in others is no reason to despair or to retreat into mere private worlds. On the contrary, it should come as a relief not to have to aim at an impossible objectivity, and to rest content instead on the one hand with the honesty of recognizing one's own starting point and on the other with the relentless aim of public, rather than merely private, discourse. Exegesis needs its Van Goghs as well as its Rembrandts; perhaps even its Picassos and its Tracey Emins. Even Gollum proved to be a necessary companion on the road to the Dark Tower. This is not to say that there is no distinction between good exegesis and bad, between good history and bad, between good theology and bad. It is to accept that such distinctions are probably less easy to draw than we have traditionally imagined, and to embark on a course of simultaneously arguing as strongly as we can for a point of view and accepting cheerfully that it may be not just inadequate – we can take that for granted – but in some respects at least quite misleading. In this as in much else I take my hat off to Ernst Käsemann, who in the preface to his greatest work declared that, having arrived at the limits set for him, he accepted the provisional nature of his own thought and deeds, and was willingly leaving the way clear for others.[8] When I first read that I thought he was wimping out, backing off from the real challenge. Now I see that he was responding to a far greater one.

But if our own positions are thus to be relativized, it may be high time to enquire about some of the supposed 'fixed points' of scholarship which, growing as they did out of a very different era to our own, may perhaps have been allowed to remain more by fashion (and the fear of being thought unscholarly if one challenges such fashion) than by solid argument. Take, for example, the widespread assumption still common in many quarters that not only Ephesians but also Colossians are not written by Paul himself, even if they may contain some material that goes back to him. There are, of course, many interesting points to be made on this subject. But our suspicions ought to be aroused by the fact that such consensus as there has ever been on the subject came from the time when the all-dominant power in New Testament scholarship lay with a particular kind of German existentialist Lutheranism for whom any ecclesiology other than a purely functional one, any view of Judaism other than a purely negative one, any view of Jesus Christ other than a fairly low Christology, any view of creation other than a Barthian 'Nein', was deeply suspect. The false either/or, as I would see it, of justification *or* the church, of salvation *or* creation, hovered as a brooding presence over the smaller arguments (which are in any case always unconvincing, given the very small textual base) from style. The extremely marked stylistic difference between 1 Corinthians and 2 Corinthians is far greater than that between, say, Romans and Ephesians, but nobody supposes for that reason that one of them is not by Paul. In particular, the assumption that a high Christology must mean later, and non-Pauline, authorship has been brought to the material, not discovered within it. And the argument recently advanced (in North America particularly) that Ephesians and Colossians are secondary *because they move away from confrontation with the Empire to collaboration with it* is frankly absurd. Much of the 'new perspective' writing on Paul has simply assumed and carried on the critical decisions reached by the old perspective, without noticing that the new perspective itself calls several of them into question. In an image suggested by Robert Morgan thirty years ago, there comes a time when the chess pieces have to be put back on the board so that the game may restart.[9] I suggest that when it comes to the extent of the Pauline corpus we may have reached that time. The same goes, I suggest, for the question of the Pauline material in Acts. These programmatic remarks, however, are for a wider purpose than this book, since though I shall draw from time to time on Ephesians, Colossians and indeed occasionally Acts, most of my substantive proposals will rest on the commonly acknowledged letters. And if that sounds as though I am urging others to put their heads over the parapet while being unwilling to do so myself, my only excuse is that I suppose that at some point I have to conform to the episcopal stereotype, even though I hope to deconstruct it in most other places.

While locating our discussion within our own culture, a further word is necessary about the perennial tension between centre and periphery, or between abstract theology and occasional or situational writings. I regard these, too, as false either/or distinctions, generated more, I think, by elements within our own culture and perhaps even our personalities, elements which incline some towards systematic statement and others towards a freewheeling and cheerfully inconsistent situational response. One sometimes meets, among biblical scholars, an innate suspicion of systematic theology which derives more, I fear, from memory of the little systems of the Sunday school than from direct acquaintance with the rich and subtle world of actual contemporary systematics. One sometimes meets the opposite, too: a suspicion of situationalism generated more by a fear of moral chaos than by a working knowledge of actual historical exegesis.

2

Creation and Covenant

1. Creation and Covenant in the Old Testament

What I mean by 'creation and covenant' will become clear if we consider a couple of psalms where the two are joined together. What I intend by using that pair of evocative terms as an initial way in to Paul will then become clear if we consider three central passages in which the same themes play the same kind of roles. This will open the way to a more detailed consideration of what, I shall argue, must be regarded as part of the fundamental structure of his thought, and how it relates to the other themes which will occupy us in subsequent chapters.

The first psalm is Psalm 19, a spectacular poem made more so by Joseph Haydn: 'The heavens are telling the glory of God.' But Haydn's setting, which never got beyond verse 1, can actually distract us from what the writer is doing. The psalm isn't just a poem about the glory of creation. It divides into two more or less equal halves (vv. 1–6 and 7–14), and it is the juxtaposition of these which opens the door to the view of creation and covenant which, I shall suggest, remains at the heart of Judaism and, as I shall argue, was always central for Paul.

The first six verses are a paean of praise to God for his creation, celebrating the fact that creation itself praises God and declares his glory without speech or language but yet with great power and force. 'Their sound has gone out into all the world, and their words to the ends of the earth.' Within this, the psalmist celebrates the power and strength of the sun. 'Nothing is hidden', he declares, 'from its searching heat.' Then, without warning, he switches to the second half of the poem, which is a similar paean of praise for Torah, the Law of YHWH. Torah does in human life what the sun does within creation: it brings the light, power and searching, probing heat of YHWH's presence into the depths of the human heart. Torah is, of course, the covenant charter of Israel, the Law given to bind Israel to YHWH, to establish the nation as his people. With Torah as its guide, Israel is the unique, chosen people of the one creator God. The same point is made graphically at the end of Psalm 147: YHWH, the creator, declares his statutes and ordinances to Israel, but he has not done so with any other nation, and they have no knowledge of his laws (147.19–20). The 'Alleluia' which concludes the psalm indicates well enough how creation and covenant sit together: Israel celebrates its unique vocation as the creator's chosen people, the people who know the secrets of the universe and are called to live by its otherwise hidden rules, while the other nations blunder around in darkness.

The second psalm I cite for my main point has a very different mood, but the same underlying theology. Psalm 74 is a lament, a complaint against the powerful heathen nations who have ravaged Jerusalem. 'O God, why have you cast us off forever; why does your anger smoke against the sheep of your pasture? . . . Your enemies have roared within your holy place, they have set up their banners there, and have hacked down all the carved work with axes and hammers . . . How long, O Lord? Why don't you do something?'

Then in verse 12 (those who relish the Anglican choral tradition will know that this moment invites a change of chant from a lament in a minor key to a strong statement in a major key) the psalmist appeals over the head of the powerful pagan nations to the creator God, the God by whose power Israel came out of Egypt. 'Yet God is my king of old; you divided the sea by your power, you broke the heads of Leviathan in the waters . . . Yours is the day, yours also is the night, you have established the light and the sun; you have fixed the boundaries of the earth, you have made summer and winter.' When everything is tottering and crashing all around, in other words, look back to Genesis 1, and to the evidences that the creator's power has in the past been made known on Israel's behalf. Then the psalm can return to the lament in verse 18, and complain: 'Remember this, O YHWH, how the enemy scoffs, how a foolish people blaspheme your name.'

Two very different psalms, each drawing on the same theology of creation and covenant. The one celebrates creation, and within that celebrates Torah as the covenant charter designed to enable each individual Israelite to become a whole, cleansed, integrated human being; the other complains that the pagans are laying Israel waste, and invokes the covenant God as also the creator God who has the power, the right and the responsibility to deal with evil. There are many other examples, but I choose these both because they are so graphic and clear, and because they point to some of the themes which I shall propose as central for Paul.

A good deal of the Old Testament could of course be brought alongside at this point. I draw attention here simply to passages to which Paul himself appeals. I have argued elsewhere that the book of Genesis demands to be read in this way: the promises to Abraham echo the commands to Adam, and the whole argument of the book, the whole point of the narrative, is that God has called Abraham and his family to undo the sin of Adam, even though Abraham and his family are themselves part of the problem as well as the bearers of the solution.[1] That, indeed, is close to the heart of Paul's own fresh reading of Genesis, as we shall see. Deuteronomy, and particularly its long exposition of the covenant in chapters 27—30, brings together creation and covenant in terms of the Land: if Israel obeys the voice of YHWH, the created order within the promised land will be abundantly fruitful, but if Israel disobeys, the Land itself will turn against them, and ultimately drive them out into exile, whence they will only return if they turn back to YHWH with all their heart and soul. Isaiah 40—55 brings together creation and covenant from one angle after another, invoking YHWH in chapter 40 as the sovereign creator in whom Israel can have complete trust and confidence, celebrating in chapter 55 the way in which his Word has the same effect, in terms of restoring Israel, as the rain and the snow which make the earth fruitful. In between, not least in the steady build-up to the final Servant Song, the prophet does what Psalms 19 and 74 and many others do:

> I, I am he that comforts you; why then are you afraid of a mere mortal who must die?
>
> You have forgotten YHWH, your maker, who stretched out the heavens and laid the foundations of the earth.
>
> You fear continually all day long because of the fury of the oppressor; but where is the oppressor's fury? The oppressed shall speedily be released;
>
> For I am YHWH your God, who stirs up the sea so that its waves roar – YHWH of hosts is his name.

> I have put my words in your mouth, and hidden you in the shadow of my hand,
> Stretching out the heavens and laying the foundations of the earth, and saying to Zion, 'You are my people'.[2]

There you have it: the creator God is the covenant God, and vice versa; and his word, particularly through his prophet and/or servant, will rescue and deliver his people from the enemy. This combination constituted the deep implicit narrative within which the multiple other narratives of second-Temple Judaism find their coherence and meaning. We could put it like this, in a double statement which might seem paradoxical but which carried deep meaning through ancient Judaism.

First, the covenant is there to solve the problems within creation. God called Abraham to solve the problem of evil, the problem of Adam, the problem of the world. (That, incidentally, is why accounts of the problem of evil which fail to incorporate covenant theology are doomed before they start; but that is another story.) Israel's calling is to hold fast by the covenant. Through Israel, God will address and solve the problems of the world, bringing justice and salvation to the ends of the earth – though quite how this will happen remains, even in Isaiah, more than a little mysterious.

But, second, creation is invoked to solve the problems within the covenant. When Israel is in trouble, and the covenant promises themselves seem to have come crashing to the ground, the people cry to the covenant God precisely as the creator. Israel goes back to Genesis 1, and to the story of the Exodus, in order to pray and trust that YHWH will do again what, as creator, he has the power and the right to do, and what as the covenant God he has the responsibility to do, namely, to establish justice in the world and, more especially, to vindicate his people when they cry to him for help. In both cases, we should note carefully, it is assumed that something has gone badly wrong. Something is deeply amiss with creation, and within that with humankind itself, something to which the covenant with Israel is the answer. Something is deeply amiss with the covenant, whether Israel's sins on the one hand or Gentile oppression on the other, or perhaps both – and to this the answer is a re-invoking of creation, or rather of God as creator.

So far I have concentrated on the Old Testament itself, partly because these themes are so clear there and partly because Paul constantly goes back to the Old Testament, not least to Genesis, Deuteronomy, the Psalms and Isaiah, not to find proof-texts for abstract ideas but in order to reground the controlling narrative, the historical story, of God, the world, humankind and Israel. But it is of course important that we also contextualize Paul in his own day by noticing these same themes in second-Temple literature. There is no space to expound this in detail. I merely note that in very different writings, such as the Wisdom of Solomon, the Qumran literature and the apocalyptic writings such as 4 Ezra and *2 Baruch*, we find exactly these themes, albeit deployed in very different ways. We find, not least, these themes invoked as the reason why Israel's God, the creator, must eventually engage in a final showdown with the forces of evil, a dramatic event which will be like the Exodus in some respects and in other respects like a great court scene, a trial in which the powers of evil are judged, condemned and overthrown. We think, most obviously, of Daniel 7 and the reuse of that passage in various later texts. Though Paul appeals over the heads of the later texts to the Bible itself, his own reuse of the biblical themes possesses an easily recognizable family likeness to the other reuses of his day.

One of the great slogans in which all this theology of creation and covenant is summed up, one with of course enormous significance at the heart of Paul's thought, is *tsedaqah elohim*, the 'righteousness' or 'justice' or 'covenant faithfulness' of God. The problem of how to translate this phrase is acute already in Isaiah and elsewhere, as it is in Paul. Somehow we need a word which will pull together this entire complex of thought, which will evoke for us what the Hebrew phrase, and then its Greek equivalent (*dikaiosynē theou*), evoked in Paul's day as it had done for a long time before: the fact that the creator and covenant God can be relied upon to act in accordance with his creating power and his covenant fidelity, to put the world to rights. How can all this be summed up in a word?

There is no such word in English. One might say 'faithfulness', but it hardly carries the sense of 'justice', of putting things to rights. One might say 'righteousness', but people inevitably hear it today either in the sense of 'ethical uprightness' or in the (to my mind mistaken) familiar Reformed understandings of it as the status which God imputes to the faithful, about which I shall say more later on. The word 'justice' itself evokes that element of what Paul, and the texts on which he drew, was talking about which is all too often forgotten today, namely that because God is the creator he has the obligation to put the world to rights once and for all, but unless we constantly remind ourselves that in the Jewish context, and in Paul himself, this 'justice' springs not from some abstract ideal but from the creator's obligation to the creation and from the covenant God's obligation to be faithful to his promises, it will lose its flavour and force. This multiple obligation is what Psalm 74 appeals to, and it is what makes sense of the actual flow of Paul's own thought in passage after passage. The word 'justice' has one advantage, though, namely that it is cognate with 'justification', the moment in the present time when one part of the creation is put to rights in advance of the final renewal. But, again, more of that anon. We are dealing in the present chapter with fundamental structures of thought, not with detailed outworking.

2. Paul: Three Central Passages

So much for the setting. I now turn to Paul to look briefly at three passages about which I have written extensively elsewhere but which I invoke at this point to demonstrate the way in which, in some of his most central arguments, the recognizable family likeness of a theology of creation and covenant reappears, albeit transposed into some different keys. I hope it is clear, by the way, that throughout what I have said so far I am using the word 'covenant', just as indeed I am using the word 'creation', not because that word occurs in all of the passages I have mentioned (in fact, it is quite rare), but because it is the most convenient shorthand I know to sum up the way in which Jews not least in Paul's day thought about themselves as the one chosen people of the creator God. At this point at least I am fully on the side of E. P. Sanders when he argues that the covenant is the hidden presupposition of Jewish literature even when the word hardly occurs.[3] Exegesis needs the concordance, but it cannot be ruled by it. It is no argument against calling Paul a covenantal theologian to point out the scarcity of *diathēkē* in his writings. We have to learn to recognize still more important things, such as implicit narratives and allusions to large biblical themes. Just because we cannot so easily look them up in a reference book that does not make them irrelevant.

(i) Colossians 1.15–20

The first Pauline passage I invoke, controversially of course in terms of authorship, is Colossians 1.15–20. I think it, and the whole letter, were written by Paul; if someone other than Paul wrote it, quoting an earlier poem, it is of course possible that the poem was written by Paul and incorporated by the anonymous letter-writer. But this is a point where such arguments fall away, I believe, in the face of theological exegesis. The poem exhibits all the traces of Paul's own thought, even though summed up uniquely in this passage; and – my main point at the moment – it also exhibits exactly that combination of creation and covenant which we have noticed in the Old Testament.[4]

Like Psalm 19, the poem falls into two halves, which are closely balanced. 'He', that is, the Messiah, 'is the image of the invisible God, the firstborn of all creation; for in him all things were created, in heaven and on earth; all things were made through him and for him' (1.15–16). He is then 'the beginning, the first-born from the dead; for in him God's fulness was pleased to dwell, and through him God reconciled all things to himself' (1.18b–20; vv. 17–18a form a smaller sequence within this larger one). Whoever wrote this was making more or less exactly the same point, by means of the poetic structure itself, as Psalm 19: the creator God is also the redeeming, covenant God, and vice versa.

The main difference, of course, is the breathtaking insertion, into this theology, of Jesus the Messiah as the one through whom both creation and redemption have come about. The echoes of Jewish wisdom-theology are part of the clue to how this has been rethought. But the crucial thing, as has often been noticed, is the way in which the poem exploits the meaning of 'in the beginning' from Genesis 1.1 itself, turning the Hebrew word for 'beginning' this way and that (beginning, head, sum total, and first fruits), and combining it with the assertion that Jesus is the true image of God, in other words, the true fulfilment of Genesis 1.26f. And of course if Jesus is the point at which creation and covenant come together, one of the most striking innovations, completely consistent with all of Paul's thought, is that this coming together has taken the form of an actual event, an event which has already happened, an event which consisted, surprisingly and shockingly, of the shameful and cruel death by crucifixion of the one who has thus fulfilled the double divine purpose. The explosive force of Paul's theology lies just here, that in both the structure of his thought and its explicit sentences he writes simultaneously of fulfilment and of something radically new – something shocking, something until that point unthinkable.

(ii) 1 Corinthians 15

This same blend of the fulfilment and the unthinkable characterizes the second passage I here highlight, namely 1 Corinthians 15. It is easy to get lost in the multiple complexities of this, one of Paul's longest and most detailed arguments.[5] But one of the key guiding principles to understanding the whole passage is that it is, at a fundamental level, an appeal to Genesis 1—3 in the light of the events concerning Jesus. I have spelled this out in more detail elsewhere, but we can summarize the point like this. As soon as the argument gets going in verse 20, Paul evokes Genesis 3: since death came through a human being, the resurrection has come by a human being; for as in Adam all die, so in the Messiah all shall be made alive. This is a statement of new creation through the Messiah, and it is developed by means of a detailed argument, in verses 23–28, drawing on various Old Testament texts not least Psalm 8, itself an evocation of Genesis 1. This leads Paul, after a short excursion (vv. 29–34), to address the question about what sort of a thing the resurrection body will be; and, in answering this crucial question, he draws on several parts of Genesis, about the seed and the plant and the different types of created physicality, that of stars and fish and animals, objects in the sky and objects on earth. This leads him in verses 42–49 to a climactic statement of the new type of resurrected physicality that has come to birth with Jesus' resurrection, contrasted with what is said of Adam in Genesis 2.7. Adam was from the earth, and earthy, whereas the new body which Jesus now possesses is a fresh gift from heaven. The end result is the creation of a new type of human beings, once more in the image of God but now, more specifically, in the image of the risen Messiah: as we have born the image of the earthly human being, we shall also bear the image of the heavenly one.

This is how the problem within the existing creation, namely sin and death,[6] has been dealt with through the Messiah, more specifically through the way in which the Messiah has been the means of fulfilling the promises of a great victory through which evil would be overthrown. This obviously looks on to the theme of our next chapter (Messiah and Apocalyptic), but it is no bad thing that we grasp already the connections between ideas that have often been played off against one another. For the moment my point is that, like the Psalms or Daniel, Paul is going back to creation itself, to Genesis, and is showing how God's fulfilment of the covenant promises has established creation's renewal. This in turn is of vital importance for understanding what 1 Corinthians 15 is all about: not the abandonment of creation, but its renewal.

(iii) Romans 1—11

The third passage is a longer one, and in taking the risk of expounding it in one go I am conscious that I am asking my readers to hold a large and complicated argument in mind all at once; but I think it is worth the effort. The passage in question is the letter to the Romans, especially the first three of its four main sections (chs. 1—11). Let me work through with a bird's eye view and propose a way of understanding Paul's masterpiece in which the twin themes of creation and covenant come to their spectacular fresh expression.[7]

In 1.18—4.25, the first major section of the letter, Paul launches in with an exposition of God's goodness and power in creation, as a way of calling the human race to account for not recognizing God and giving him the praise and honour that were his due. As a result, image-bearing human beings have become corrupt; violence and hatred fills the world; and even those who think they are above such things are themselves in fact no better. To this scenario, in which Paul hardly differs from many of his Jewish contemporaries, the Jew would answer – Saul of Tarsus himself would have answered! – with a statement of the covenant: God has called Israel to be the light to the nations, the teacher of the foolish, the guide to the blind. That is what the covenant was there for. But when Paul sees this argument coming he turns it, too, on its head (2.17–29): the covenant people have become part of the problem, not the agents of the solution. Israel is no better than the nations, as is proved by biblical texts which speak of exile. This creates a crisis for God himself, a crisis exactly parallel to the crisis which 4 Ezra saw so painfully: how is God to be both faithful to the covenant and just in his dealings with the whole creation?

This is precisely the question of the *dikaiosynē theou*, the faithful covenant justice of God, which Paul had announced as the letter's main theme in 1.17. And, beginning in 3.21, he provides a fresh answer to the question, an answer not available to writers like 4 Ezra: God has unveiled his *dikaiosynē* in the faithful Messiah, Jesus, the one in whom at last we find an Israelite faithful to God's purpose, the one through whose death sin has been dealt with, the one through whom God has now called into being a renewed people among whom Jews and Gentiles are welcome on equal terms. Creation and covenant then come together with great force in chapter 4, for which Genesis 15 as a whole is foundational: Paul is recalling Abraham, neither as a random proof-text for justification by faith, nor as an example of a Christian before Christ, but precisely as the one with whom God made the covenant in the first place, the covenant which has now been fulfilled in Jesus. It is with Romans 4, as much as with 3.21–31, that we see the unveiling of the *dikaiosynē theou*.

But this covenant fulfilment, through which Jew and Gentile come together as the true children of Abraham (that is the main theme of Romans 4), is also, implicitly, the renewal of creation after the disaster outlined in chapter 1. As has often been shown, the faith of Abraham as spelled out in 4.18–21 constitutes the deliberate reversal of the unbelief of humankind in Romans 1. Abraham looked at his good-as-dead body, but did not grow weak in faith; he didn't waver in unbelief; he grew strong in faith, giving God the glory, believing completely that God, as creator, had the power to do what he had promised. That is why, as an advance sign of creation's restoration, and with it the restoration of the male-and-female nature of image-bearing humankind, Abraham and Sarah are enabled to bear a son. Abraham's faith thus points forwards appropriately to the death and resurrection of Jesus, and this faith becomes the covenant marker, the badge of God's multi-ethnic people, the sign of God's renewed humanity. Furthermore, one of the tell-tale signs of what Paul is thinking in this chapter as he expounds Genesis 15 is his redefinition, his broadening, of the promise of God to Abraham. In Genesis, Abraham is promised the Holy Land. For Paul, as for some others in his day, this was to be interpreted as an advance sign of something else. The promise to Abraham and his family, declares Paul, was that he should inherit the *world* (4.13).

This is the promise which is then taken up in the next four chapters. Romans 1—4 expounds, from one point of view, the way in which the problem of creation has been addressed by the fulfilment of the covenant, while simultaneously the problem of the covenant (the failure of ethnic Israel) has been dealt with by God's action through Jesus the Messiah, in fulfilment of the promise of new creation. Chapters 5—8 develop the themes of creation and covenant in a closely related manner. Romans 5, densely but deftly, outlines like 1 Corinthians 15 the way in which the obedience of the one man Jesus the Messiah has more than reversed the effects of the one man Adam. He has done, it seems, what the covenant was put in place to do. But what has happened to the covenant itself?

This is the problem of the Jewish Law, which comes to its head especially in Romans 7. (This context of creation and covenant, I might add, is the right way to approach the question of 'Paul and the Law', rather than the approaches common within a non-creational or non-covenantal reading.) In Romans 7, Paul expounds what happened when the Torah arrived in Israel, and what happens still as Israel lives under the Torah; and he does so in such a way as to make it clear that, through Torah, Israel actually recapitulates the sin of Adam and the sinful human life which follows from it. You might almost say that at this point he is deliberately deconstructing Psalm 19; or, perhaps, that he is probing its final verses and discovering that the more you embrace Torah the more it does indeed show up your secret faults. But Romans 7 is then answered, of course, by Romans 8, which is Paul's most spectacular piece of creation-theology, a bursting out of a fresh reading of Genesis 1—3, coupled with the Exodus narrative of liberation from slavery and the journey to the promised inheritance: creation itself will be set free from its bondage to decay, to share the freedom of the glory of God's children. And the fulcrum around which the argument turns is Romans 8.3–4. God has done what the Torah, weakened by the flesh, could not do: that is, God has accomplished the goals for which the covenant was put in place, while dealing simultaneously with the fact that the covenant people themselves were part of the problem within creation. Through Jesus and the Spirit there is therefore covenant renewal, which results, as you would expect once you locate Paul within an overarching Jewish narrative of creation and covenant, in new creation. That is the underlying logic of Romans 7 and 8.

Romans 9 begins with a lament which reminds us, after a fashion, of Psalm 74. Israel is in dire straits, having failed to believe in its own Messiah when he came, and having continued that failure by the refusal to accept the gospel about him preached by Paul and the other apostles. Paul's wrestling with this problem takes the form, principally, of a retelling of the covenant narrative, a retelling which we can plot on the grid of other similar retellings in the second-Temple literature, though it goes beyond the parallels in various striking ways. As gradually becomes clear, this is of course an account precisely of the *dikaiosynē theou*, God's faithful covenant justice, which seems to be called into question both by what has now happened and indeed by the nature of the promises in the first place (Isaac not Ishmael, Jacob not Esau, and so on). Israel, declares Paul (10.3–4), was ignorant of God's covenant justice, and sought to establish its own status of covenant membership, of being-in-the-right, and so did not submit to God's covenant plan, the plan which came to its goal in the Messiah.

Paul then articulates, in a spectacular and commonly misunderstood passage, the covenant renewal which has taken place.[8] In 10.6–10 he expounds Deuteronomy 30, the passage which spoke of return from exile, of restoration after covenant judgment, a passage already expounded in parallel ways by the very different books of Baruch on the one hand and 4QMMT on the other. 'Do not say in your heart, who shall ascend into heaven, or go down to the depths, to bring the Torah near to you; the word is near you, on your lips and in your heart.' Paul expounds this statement of covenant renewal in relation to what God has done in Christ and by the Spirit (not mentioned explicitly but certainly presupposed in this passage). And the result is that now, instead of the return of ethnic Israel to the Holy Land, as envisaged in Deuteronomy, the message goes out to all people. As in Romans 8, the whole world has become the Holy Land, claimed through the gospel of Jesus the Messiah on behalf of the creator God. This is the point where Paul triumphantly quotes Psalm 19: their sound has gone out into all the world, and their words to the ends of the earth. The apostolic mission simply follows the line of the original gospel, the good news of the first creation itself. Covenant renewal has resulted in the reclaiming of the created order. As he says in Colossians 1.23 (referring, I think, to the unspoken shock wave that ran through the whole cosmos at Easter), the gospel has already been proclaimed to all the world, and he, Paul, has the job of being its servant. When human beings come to believe this gospel they are precisely the first-fruits of redeemed creation; the phrase is that of James (1.18), but on this occasion at least the sentiment tallies exactly with that of Paul. Abraham and his seed are indeed to inherit the world, but Abraham's family has been redefined around Jesus as Israel's Messiah.

This hint of creation renewed through covenant renewal bursts out at the end of Romans 11, where Paul echoes some of the Old Testament's grandest celebrations of God as the wise, inscrutable creator:

> O, the depth of the riches and the wisdom and the knowledge of God!
> How unsearchable are his judgments, how inscrutable are his ways.
> For from him and through him and to him are all things.
> To him be glory for ever, Amen.

By coming to a fresh understanding of God's faithful covenant justice, displayed in the story of Israel reshaped around Jesus the Messiah, Paul has arrived back at a primal, characteristically Jewish, praise of God the creator.

These three passages, from Colossians, 1 Corinthians and Romans, offer strong prima facie evidence that we are indeed right to read Paul in terms of that theology of creation and covenant we find in the Old Testament. But, as we have seen, for him it is always a matter of going from creation to new creation, and from covenant to renewed covenant. Fulfilment and surprising renewal are the constant thematic notes.

Further examples abound. It would be interesting to explore the way in which, in 2 Corinthians 3—5, the theology of new covenant in chapter 3 works its way through to new creation in 5.17 ('if anyone is in the Messiah – new creation!'), and to the claim in 5.19 that God was in the Messiah reconciling the *world* to himself. Similarly, Galatians 3 and 4, in which as in Romans the promises to Abraham are explored in relation to their fulfilment through Jesus the Messiah, lead Paul to declare in 6.14–16 that because of the cross of Jesus the world has been crucified to him, and he to the world, since now neither circumcision nor uncircumcision matters, but only new creation. This is the rule, the *kanōn*, by which God's renewed people must walk, claiming as they do the title of 'Israel of God'. And when we start drawing out these themes, the entire argument of Ephesians 1—3 begins to clamour to be included, whoever we think wrote it.

I have now made the case for saying that the themes of creation and covenant, rooted in the Old Testament and developed within second-Temple Judaism, remained basic within the very Jewish thought of Paul. We can see him developing them in various ways, but he has not abandoned them in favour of some different overarching scheme. In particular, as we have seen, he believes that Israel's God, the creator, has acted decisively to fulfil the covenant promises and so to renew both covenant and creation. Paul thereby understands himself to be living at a different moment in the story, though there are partial parallels within the inaugurated eschatology we find at Qumran. The new age has already begun, though the old age continues alongside it. That in turn generates both Paul's vision of the church and the problems he addresses within it, but of that we must speak elsewhere.

What I want to do now, in drawing together the threads of this chapter, is to show how the twin themes of creation and covenant offer a context, an implicit narrative, within which we can grasp Paul's understanding of what has gone wrong in the world and in Israel and how it is put right – of, if you like, evil on the one hand and grace on the other. This will enable us to see how the questions of justification and soteriology are better approached from this angle than the normal ones, a line we shall continue to pursue in subsequent chapters. We will then be able to suggest, in conclusion, that his central picture of Jesus, more especially his death and resurrection, answers closely to the biblical images of creation and covenant with which we began.

3. Evil and Grace, Plight and Solution

As we saw earlier, the implicit narrative of covenant always presupposed that something had gone drastically wrong within creation. But it isn't just that if God is proposing a solution there must have been something wrong. The particular solution God proposes – that of beginning a family and promising them a land – shows that what is wrong concerns, in a central way, the fracturing of human relationships and the fracturing of the relationship between humans and the non-human creation. And the particular faith for which God calls indicates, as Romans 4 draws out, that at the core of the problem is the failure of humans to trust God, to give him praise and honour as the all-powerful creator. All of this is strikingly re-emphasized in the gift of Torah, which holds out an extraordinary blueprint of what a genuinely human life is like, a blueprint which called forth the delighted acclaim we noted in Psalm 19, and of course plenty of other places.

The failure of human beings to be the truly image-bearing creatures God intended results, therefore, in corruption and death. When we begin with creation, and with God as creator, we can see clearly that the frequently repeated warnings about sin and death, referred to as axiomatic by Paul, are not arbitrary, as though God were simply a tyrant inventing odd laws and losing his temper with those who flouted them, but structural: humans were made to function in particular ways, with worship of the creator as the central feature, and those who turn away from that worship – that is, the whole human race, with a single exception – are thereby opting to seek life where it is not to be found, which is another way of saying that they are courting their own decay and death. This is to say, with the entire Jewish tradition, that the basic sin is idolatry, the worship of that which is not in fact the living creator God.

All this contextualizes one of Paul's key technical terms, *sarx*, normally translated 'flesh'. As is well known, Paul does *not* mean by 'flesh' simply physical substance. For that he normally uses *sōma*, usually translated 'body'. For him, the word 'flesh' is a way of denoting material within the corruptible world and drawing attention to the fact that it is precisely corruptible, that it will decay and die. From that point Paul's usage expands one more level, to include the moral behaviour which, consequent upon idolatry, is already a sign of, and an invitation to, that progressive corruption: hence 'the works of the flesh'. This analysis, seen from within an overall theology of the goodness of creation and the deconstruction of it through idolatry, is preferable to those accounts which approach the problem from other angles, for instance the earlier history of the word on the one hand or the assumptions of a dualist worldview on the other. The controlling narratives, in this case that of creation, are all-important.

The same is true, and this brings us to another usage of the same word *sarx*, for Paul's account of what is wrong within the covenant. Put simply, his point, repeated from several angles and in varying degrees of intensity, is that Israel too is in Adam: the people who bear the solution are themselves part of the problem, and the good and holy Torah (to its own surprise, one might almost say) simply intensifies this problem, partly by pointing at sin within Israel, and partly, at a second level, by apparently encouraging Israel to make it an idol, to use it as a way of establishing an inalienable status of national privilege. This is what Paul can refer to as Israel *according to the flesh*. This point needs spelling out more fully, but not here.

This move shows, I believe, the folly of dividing up readings of Paul into the false either/or of those on the one hand which highlight the problem of sin and the question of forgiveness and those on the other which highlight the problem of Israel and the inclusion of the Gentiles within God's people. This is where the so-called 'new perspective' has made one of its necessary points – that every time Paul discusses justification he seems simultaneously to be talking about Gentile inclusion – but has not, usually, shown how this integrates with the traditional view that he is talking about how sinners are put right with God.[9] Once we frame the question within the overall narratives of creation and covenant, the way is clear and open to a fresh statement of Paul which will do far more exegetical justice to the passages concerned and which will show how these two emphases are in fact part of the same thing, both to be equally stressed.

Let me put the point in a sequence of three propositions which Paul everywhere presupposes and frequently makes explicit in whole or in part.

(1) God made the covenant with Abraham as the means of dealing with evil within the good creation, which meant dealing in particular with evil within human beings, God's image-bearers. This I have already explained.

(2) The family of Abraham, who themselves share in the evil, as well as in the image-bearing vocation, of the rest of humanity, treated their vocation to be the light of the world as indicating exclusive privilege. This was their own meta-sin, their own second-order form of idolatry, compounding the basic forms they already shared with

the Gentiles. This further point is basic to Paul's critique of Israel in such passages as Romans 2, 7 and 10 and Galatians 2, 3 and 4.

(3) When God fulfils the covenant through the death and resurrection of Jesus and the gift of the Spirit, thereby revealing his faithful covenant justice and his ultimate purpose of new creation, this has the effect *both* of fulfilling the original covenant purpose (thus dealing with sin and procuring forgiveness) *and* of enabling Abraham's family to be the worldwide Jew-plus-Gentile people it was always intended to be. Indeed, when we rightly understand the matter, we shall see that from Paul's perspective at least these two effects were so closely aligned with one another that they not only could be spoken of in the same breath but demanded to be thought of as the same thought.

If there is one major result of this chapter in terms of current debates, it is that the 'new perspective' on the one hand, and its critics on the other, both need to come to terms with the integrated vision of human sin and redemption and Israel's fall and restoration which characterizes Paul through and through, precisely because his controlling categories are creation and covenant. He is not simply assuming an implicit narrative about how individual sinners find a right relationship with a holy God (any more than he is simply assuming an implicit narrative about how Gentiles can have easy access to God's people). In so far as he would be happy with the former way of stating matters at all, he would insist on framing it within the much larger question of how the creator God can be true to creation, how the covenant God can be true to the covenant, and how those things are not two but one. And that is what the phrase *dikaiosynē theou* is all about.

If this is Paul's account of evil, and of the plight of humankind and Israel and the way God has addressed it, what can we say in summary about his account of grace? This points towards the topic of the next chapter, but we can for the moment just say this: that Paul's vision of God's action in Jesus the Messiah and by the Spirit leads him from several angles to insist that the ultimate result is new creation, in which the old is set free from corruption and decay. This is accomplished, more specifically, not just through the covenant but through the *renewal of* the covenant: Paul draws explicitly on prophetic texts of covenant renewal, not least Jeremiah 31 and Ezekiel

36, and ultimately on Deuteronomy 30 itself, arguably the basis of the whole idea. In both creation and covenant, grace perfects or completes nature not simply by topping it up but by judging it, condemning the evil which has infected it, and then renewing it. This, of course, is precisely the model offered by the representative death of Jesus the Messiah, who from Paul's perspective offered to God the perfect obedience Israel should have offered, and thereby fulfilled on behalf of Israel as well as the world the rescue operation the covenant had always envisaged. Once more, if we approach Paul as a theologian of creation and covenant, we will not fall into the trap of so much exegesis, which has marginalized his theme of new creation and has forgotten altogether that the point of justification, and of Abraham and his family, always was that the way God intended to deal with evil was through keeping the promises made in the covenant.

4. Conclusion: Jesus within Creation and Covenant

Throughout this chapter I have spoken exclusively of Paul within his Jewish context. What has happened to his other two worlds? Part of the answer is that by sketching Paul as a theologian of creation and covenant we are insisting that it was this essentially Jewish message which he announced in the pagan world, and which was, for him (as for, say, the Wisdom of Solomon), the clue to the divine wisdom which upstaged the wisdom of the world. It would indeed be possible, from the point we have now reached, to glance across at the Areopagus address in Acts 17.22–31 and to show that its deconstruction of Stoic, Epicurean and Academician theologies is fully in line with what we have found in Paul himself. (Indeed, I suspect that it is the failure of previous generations to come to terms with Paul's theology of creation and covenant that has made them wonder whether the Paul of Acts 17 is compatible with the Paul of the letters.) And from there we could show that it is precisely through his theology of a renewed covenant, in which all the nations can share on equal terms, and of a new creation, in which the whole world is already claimed by the creator as the new, extended and soon-to-be-redeemed Holy Land, that Paul is able to launch his opposition to the worldwide claims of Caesar's empire with those of Jesus the Messiah, the world's true Lord. But these are themes for later on. I conclude the present chapter by going back to Psalms 19 and 74 and suggesting that, for Paul, the questions they raise have now been dealt with through the death and resurrection of Jesus.

The celebration of creation and of Torah in Psalm 19 leads the psalmist, as we saw, to the slightly anxious prayer that he may be kept from presumptuous sin. Creation summons him to worship, Torah to obedience, but in both he may fall short. Paul sees that humans have indeed fallen short, and that Torah has simply exacerbated that problem within Israel. But in Colossians 1, and Romans 7 and 8, we see Paul's answer. God has done what Torah could not. The one through whom all things were made is the one through whom all things are redeemed.

More tellingly still, we can line up the agony and the faith of Psalm 74 with that of Paul as he faces in Romans 9—11 the plight of his fellow Jews. But we can look wider as well, to the whole story of the gospel which underlies everything Paul says and does. In the psalmist's agony at the destroyed Temple, and his strong affirmation of God as creator, we glimpse exactly the same theological structure as we find in the crucifixion of Jesus by the pagans and God's answer by raising him from the dead as the beginning of the renewal of all creation. Once we hold creation and covenant in our minds as the framework of the picture, we find that not only sin and redemption but also Christology itself come into fresh focus, a focus we shall explore further as this book goes on.

But we have already said enough to indicate that for Paul the theology of creation and covenant constantly drew him forward to the events concerning Jesus, events shocking both in their very nature and being unexpected. It is as the fulfilment of creation and covenant, not in their abolition, that we find ourselves compelled to turn our full attention, in the next chapter in this book, to the second pair of themes around which Paul's thought was organized: Messiah and apocalyptic.

3

Messiah and Apocalyptic

1. Introduction

'When I first came to you,' says Paul to the Corinthians, 'I determined that I would know nothing among you except Jesus the Messiah, and him crucified.'[1] We may doubt, in view of everything else he says he taught them first time around, just how restrictive this was – just as, when we read the Areopagus address in Acts 17, we may legitimately doubt whether Paul, given the chance to speak to the greybeards in Athens, would have limited himself to a breathless two-minute summary critique of paganism. In particular, 1 Corinthians 15 makes it clear that when Paul said he focused on Jesus as the crucified Messiah, he didn't mean that he didn't talk about the resurrection, as some have wrongly imagined. But in this chapter, as we continue our study of Paul's central and controlling themes, I want to start further back, and look at the concept of Messiahship itself, and at the way in which Paul's view of Jesus as Messiah enables him both to draw on the categories of what we loosely call Jewish apocalyptic in a striking new way, and to integrate those categories, in ways often thought impossible, with those of creation and covenant at which we looked in the previous chapter. This will clear the way for a fresh presentation, in the following chapter, of what I have called a 'fresh perspective' on Paul (as opposed to the merely 'new' perspective, which is now somewhat less new than it was), in which the unveiling, or apocalypse, of the Messiah as Israel's king and therefore the world's true Lord challenges, as within Jewish thinking it was bound to do, the grand claims of pagan empire.

Both the categories I am studying in this chapter are controversial. Many writers on Paul in the last two hundred years have paid no attention whatever to the concept of Messiahship, assuming that when Paul wrote *Christos* he thought of it simply as a proper name. (Many non-scholars today, I discover, hear the phrase 'Jesus Christ' in that way, with 'Jesus' being as it were his Christian name and 'Christ' being as it were his surname, as though Jesus' parents were called Joseph Christ and Mary Christ.) Equally, there are many writers, both in New Testament studies and in systematic theology, for whom the word 'Christ' has been taken to mean, more or less straightforwardly, 'the incarnate one', 'the God/Man', 'the one who reveals God', or something else down those lines, without regard either for the Jewish meanings of 'Messiah', to which such ideas were foreign, or for Paul's own actual usage, which was both derived from Judaism and interestingly innovative. One way or another, there has been enormous resistance (despite a great deal of prima facie evidence) to any suggestion that Paul thought of Jesus as the Messiah promised by God to Israel. This itself raises questions about the context and climate of thought within which mainstream Pauline scholarship has worked, and warns us about the uphill struggle involved in any attempt to argue the opposite.

So, too, with apocalyptic. In addition to being one of the most frustrating words to type – I must have typed the word thousands of times, and it still routinely comes out wrong – this term has proved so slippery and many-sided in scholarly discourse that one is often tempted to declare a moratorium on it altogether. Books and articles continue to appear using the word in subtly different senses. I have in my proud possession a letter from Ernst Käsemann in which he declares that he understands the word 'apocalyptic' to mean neither more nor less than *Naherwartung*, 'imminent expectation', that is, the expectation of the imminent end of the world. I well remember one of my Oxford colleagues, having read my book *The New Testament and the People of God*, beginning a conversation with the words 'now that you've abandoned apocalyptic', when I had spent most of a chapter arguing carefully for a different meaning for the term, and then insisting that in this more historically justifiable sense it did indeed apply to both first-century Judaism and early Christianity. The work of such scholars as Christopher Rowland and John Collins has challenged head on the assumption that so-called 'apocalyptic' literature, and the so-called 'apocalyptic' worldview itself, was straightforwardly dualistic, expecting the end of history, the end of the space-time universe itself. But the word still functions for many scholars as a shorthand way of expressing a dualism which they see as deeply embedded within a certain type of Judaism, and deeply influential on Paul, and many have taken this underlying apocalyptic framework of Paul's thought as a clear indication that he could not and would not have embraced anything recognizable as 'covenant' theology, with its implied continuity between the old creation (and indeed the old covenant) and the new. Part of the underlying aim of the present chapter, standing alongside the previous one, is to argue for a framework of thought in Paul, dependent on similar frameworks of thought within second-Temple Judaism, within which covenant and apocalyptic, freshly understood, are mutually reinforcing rather than mutually antithetical. As an obvious initial signpost in the right direction, it would be a bold move to argue that the Essenes we glimpse in the Qumran texts were not an apocalyptic movement. But it is also obvious that their life, their faith and their hope centred upon the covenant and its renewal. That which history joins, we should not divide.

In both parts of the present chapter, then, I am attempting to turn back particular tides of opinion. These are not universal. Many scholars will be predisposed, broadly at least, to agree with me. One of the frustrating but also exciting things about today's New Testament scholarship is that there is in almost every area such a wide range of opinion that important matters which some of us take for granted as hardly needing stating, let alone proving, are regarded by others as bizarre or deeply counter-intuitive – and vice versa. I apologize, therefore, to those for whom this chapter seems to be pushing on an open door, as well as to those for whom it seems more like trying to drive a coach and horses through a solid stone wall.

2. Jesus as Messiah in Paul

First, then, the question of Jesus' Messiahship in Paul. I have argued this case elsewhere in detail but it needs at least to be summarized for our present purposes.[2] The material is scattered throughout Paul's letters, but certain features stand out clearly. It may be of interest to note that much of the evidence is 'heuristic', that is, it consists of passages of which we can say, 'If you read *Christos* here as merely a proper name, or as simply a divine title, it won't make nearly as much overall sense as if you read it as "Messiah".' (The underlying question of what counts as 'making sense' is of course one of those matters which make the intellectual quest perennially exciting.)

I understand the relevant Pauline passages within the context of the wide and sometimes bewildering variety of messianic expectations which we can trace within some, though not all, second-Temple literature. At the risk of gross over-compression, we may summarize this view in six points.[3]

First, we are talking about a *royal* Messiahship. The Messiah is Israel's true king; hence also, since Israel is the people of the one creator God, he is the world's true Lord. Paul, we should note, shows no interest in a *priestly* Messiah such as we find in some Qumran texts alongside the king. Second, the Messiah will successfully fight Israel's great and ultimate battle against the forces of evil and paganism. Third, the Messiah will build the Temple, the house to which Israel's God will at last return and live. Fourth, the Messiah will thus bring Israel's history to its climax, fulfilling the biblical texts regarded in this period as messianic prophecies, and usher in the new world of which prophets and others had spoken. Fifth, the Messiah will act in all this as Israel's representative, like David fighting Goliath on Israel's behalf. Sixth, in another sense the Messiah will act as *God's* representative or agent to Israel and hence to the world.

There is no time to spell these out, but each is attested here and there in second-Temple readings of the biblical texts, and each is, as I shall now suggest rather than argue in detail, solidly present in Paul's use of *Christos* for Jesus.[4]

We may begin with a passage which cries out to have *Christos* understood as 'Messiah'. Romans 9.5 is often cited as the most obvious example of this phenomenon: at the end of a list of the privileges of the Jewish people, Paul declares that 'of their race, according to the flesh, is *ho Christos*'. (I should say, before going any further, that the use of the definite article in relation to *Christos*, though important, doesn't get us very far, because Greek uses the article in subtly different ways to English. We must beware of easy but false assumptions at this point.) But once we grant Romans 9.5, we open the question of how that verse functions as an introduction to the argument which is to come, and indeed in parallel to other introductory formulaic statements in Romans. Within Romans 9—11, it is often not noticed that Paul's large-scale argument consists of a retelling of the story of Israel, from Abraham, Isaac and Jacob through Moses and the Exodus to the prophets and the exile . . . and then, with a glance at the remnant, to the Messiah. *Telos gar nomou Christos* in Romans 10.4 ('the Messiah is the . . . end? goal? of the law') relates directly both to 9.5 and to the whole narrative of which it forms the climax – and 'climax' is in fact a good translation for *telos* here. The entire narrative is, arguably, messianic from start to finish, in the sense that Paul understands the story of Israel to be reaching its climax with the coming and achievement of the Messiah, corresponding to the fourth sense of 'Messiah' noted above.

But if we grant Romans 9.5, even without the more contentious interpretation of what follows, we must also notice Romans 1.3–4, the one Pauline passage outside the Pastorals which mentions David specifically as Jesus' ancestor. Of course, this passage has routinely been marginalized, and treated as though it were a mere throwaway introductory line, designed to curry favour with Jewish Christians in Rome for whom such ideas were still important while for Paul, of course, they were not. But there are four arguments which tell very strongly against this. First, we know from many of Paul's letters that his opening passages are often carefully crafted with an eye to what he wants to say in the rest of the letter. It seems very unlikely that he would place in such a prominent position an explicit statement of something he regarded as at best inadequate and at worst misleading. Second, what Paul says about Jesus as the letter develops, not least in chapters 6—8, can be seen as drawing out the implications of this opening statement, not simply of the passage more usually said to be thematic, namely 1.16–17. Third, Paul seems to be alluding to various biblical passages (Psalm 2 and 2 Samuel 7 come obviously to mind) which we know as messianic proof-texts in Qumran. Fourth, at the letter's thematic conclusion in 15.12, Paul quotes Isaiah's prophecy about 'the root of Jesse'. Again, unless we are to say that Paul chose to end his longest and most carefully structured theological argument with a quotation designed to put his readers on exactly the wrong train of thought, we find ourselves compelled to the view that he really does see the argument of Romans framed by, and hence by implication consisting in, an exposition of the Messiahship of Jesus and its meaning and effects. And, as I have argued in my commentary on Romans and in other places, when we read the letter this way it opens a great many doors which no other keys will unlock.

The same can be said of Galatians, where the long argument of chapters 3 and 4 again presents (despite what many commentators suppose) a sustained argument involving a retelling of the story of Israel. God made the initial promises to Abraham; subsequently, he gave the Law through Moses; but this was always a strictly temporary stage, designed to keep Israel under control, like a young son, until the moment of maturity. And this moment of maturity is described in terms of the coming of the Messiah, who both represents Israel and brings its history to its ordained goal.

But the theme is found much more widely than simply in Romans and Galatians. When we turn to the Corinthian correspondence we find several of the other messianic senses in full play. In the great exposition of the resurrection in 1 Corinthians 15, Paul draws on more messianic texts, this time from Psalms 8 and 110, in order to describe how Jesus as Messiah has won the great battle, not against temporal enemies, but against the entire forces of evil, culminating in death itself. The messianic battle has been redefined, not abandoned, and indeed it has been placed centrally within one of Paul's greatest arguments. In this light we return to the opening two chapters of the letter, the passage about 'Christ crucified' with which we began the present chapter, and discover that there too Paul sees Jesus involved in God's ultimate battle against 'the rulers of this age' (2.6–8). (This, by the way, indicates an important exegetical principle, in line with what I said in the previous chapter about the word 'covenant': it might be handy if we could do exegesis simply through the concordance, but it is vital that we study themes as well as words and, as here, learn to recognize a theme even though the word by which we might have expected to track it down, in this case *Christos*, does not occur in the verses in question. Since it has been central in the argument which has immediately preceded, we should not be shy of assuming that Paul wants us still to have it in mind.) This theme of the victorious battle is of course echoed in various other passages, not least Colossians 2.14–15.

Then in 1 Corinthians we find the church, and individual Christians, described as, among other things, the renewed Temple, built by God on the foundation which is Jesus the Messiah, and now indwelt by the Spirit.[5] This theme, too, is present in other passages even where the word 'Temple' is not mentioned, for instance in Romans 8.1–11, where the idea of God's indwelling Spirit resulting in the resurrection of the body is closely cognate with books such as Ezekiel in which the outpouring of God's Spirit results in covenant renewal, resurrection from the dead, return from exile, the rebuilding of the Temple and new creation. (It is to Paul, indeed, that we owe the striking insight that the Spirit's indwelling in those who belong to the Messiah constitutes in a quite new way the eschatological return of YHWH to Zion.) These rich and dense themes, as I said in the first chapter, cannot be appreciated by the kind of minimalist exegesis which tries to apply the laws of mathematics or engineering to the study of ancient texts. Exuberant writing calls for exuberant exegesis: not, of course, uncontrolled or fanciful exegesis, but an exegesis which pays attention to the proper controls, which are neither narrow lexicography nor philology, important though those are, but the wider rules of narrative discourse.

In particular, the often-studied *incorporative* use of *Christos* in Paul tells heavily in favour of a messianic reference. I suggested a long time ago that Paul was drawing on a theme present in the Old Testament though not so frequently taken up in second-Temple literature, that of the incorporative King in whom Israel is summed up. 'We have no inheritance *in David*, nor yet a share *in the son of Jesse*,' say the rebels under both David and Rehoboam.[6] We should not be surprised, returning to Romans for a moment, that when Paul starts and ends a long argument with a statement that Jesus is the true son of David, the true 'root of Jesse', a good portion of it should turn out to be an exposition of what it means to be *in the Messiah*, to belong to the people who are summed up 'in him'.

Paul's sometimes bewildering usage in relation to the words 'Jesus', 'Christ' and 'Lord' comes out very cleanly on this analysis. He routinely says that something has happened 'through Jesus', in other words, through the agency of the human being Jesus of Nazareth; but he also regularly speaks of people entering into the Messiah's people, that is, coming *into Christ*, as a result of which they are now *in Christ*, so that what is true of him is true of them, and vice versa. This, obviously, is the point of Romans 6, and continues through to Romans 8. We can observe it close up in the otherwise bewildering language of Romans 8.11: if the Spirit of him who raised *Jesus* from the dead – the historical Jesus of Nazareth – dwells within you, then the one who raised *the Messiah* from the dead will give life to your mortal bodies also through the indwelling Spirit. The shorthand phrase *Iesous Christos* thus enables Paul to draw together several narratives at the heart of his thinking. God's plan for Israel and the world had come to its fulfilment in Jesus of Nazareth, Israel's Messiah and the world's true Lord, in whom Israel's destiny had been accomplished and in whom, therefore, Jew and Gentile alike could inherit the promises made to Abraham.

This theme makes it very likely, in my view, that when Paul speaks in Galatians and Romans of *pistis Christou*, he normally intends to denote the *faithfulness of the Messiah to the purposes of God* rather than the faith by which Jew and Gentile alike believe the gospel and so are marked out as God's renewed people. At the risk, again, of short-circuiting a complex current debate, I want simply to draw attention to a key moment in Romans where the argument I have advanced so far points strongly in this direction. In Romans 3.2–3 Paul declares that Israel had been *entrusted* with God's oracles; in other words, that Israel had been God's chosen messenger to the nations. But Israel, Paul says (drawing of course on the prophetic critique), had been unfaithful, had not discharged the commission. This is cognate with what he says in 10.2–3: Israel had failed to understand God's covenant purposes, and had sought to promote a covenant status for itself alone. What then is God to do? Is he to abandon the covenant and to decide, as so many theologians have proposed, on a drastically different 'plan B'? By no means: let God be true (3.4), though all human beings be false. God must stick to the plan. But that means that sooner or later he will require a representative Israelite who *will* be faithful, who will be obedient to God's purpose not only for Israel but *through* Israel for the world. The world then waits (without knowing it), and Israel then waits (with that knowing which comes to expression in prophecy and prayer) for God to unveil his purpose, to reveal how it is that he will after all be true to his covenant. But when the moment of unveiling arrives (3.21–22), what we see is God's covenant faithfulness operating *dia pisteōs Iēsou Christou*, that is, *through the faithfulness of Jesus the Messiah*. Precisely as Messiah, he offers God that representative faithfulness to the plan of salvation through which the plan can go ahead at last, Abraham can have a worldwide family (chapter 4), and the long entail of Adam's sin and death can be undone (5.12–21) through his *obedience*, which as we know from 1.5 is for Paul very closely aligned with faith, faithfulness or fidelity.

We have hereby arrived at the threshold of the second part of this chapter. But before we open the door and go in we must pause and note the final and critical point in Paul's view of Jesus as Messiah. At certain key moments (which, though not frequent, are always, when they come, central and emphatic), Paul refers to Jesus as God's son. At one level this certainly carries the messianic meaning it had for some Jewish groups of Paul's day, dependent on Psalm 2, 2 Samuel 7 and other passages like Psalm 89 where the Messiah is God's firstborn. But with Paul we begin to see that usage of 'son of God' which grows and swells within early Christianity until it has drowned out the messianic meaning almost entirely. 'When the time had fully come, God sent forth his son'; 'what the Torah could not do, God has done, sending his son in the likeness of sinful flesh'; 'if God did not spare his own son, but gave him up for us all, how will he not with him give us all things?'[7] Paul here draws on the language of Wisdom and Torah, God's gifts to his people, but translates them into the messianic terms of divine sonship, thereby creating a puzzling theological proposal for which only the later language of the Trinity would be adequate. And he thereby also completes the set of messianic themes which we noted in Judaism, albeit in a way which took a decisive step beyond anything we know from his contemporaries. The royal Messiah had come from the seed of David, had fought and won the ultimate battle, had built the new temple, had brought Israel's history to its long-prophesied climax, and had done so as Israel's representative and even as God's representative. In the light of all this the conclusion ought to be clear: Paul saw Jesus as the true Messiah promised to Israel.

Why then, we may ask, has this not been abundantly clear to exegetes and theologians? Two interconnected reasons stand out. First, as long as the dominant history-of-religions paradigm was trying to understand Paul in terms of his mission to the Gentile world and hence in terms of a 'translation' of Jewish ideas into Gentile ones, it was bound to marginalize such a centrally Jewish theme. Again and again we have been told that Paul could not have emphasized Jesus' Messiahship because it would mean nothing to a Gentile audience; hence the proposal, from Bousset through Bultmann and on even to those who in other ways do not share their agendas, that Paul dropped Messiahship in favour of other more apparently relevant themes such as *kyrios*, Lord. This fitted in with the manifest desire of such scholars to remake Paul's thought in explicitly non-Jewish categories. Even when this has been reversed, as by W. D.

Davies, E. P. Sanders, Martin Hengel and others, the potential significance of Messiahship has not been drawn out and has indeed sometimes still been resisted. Scholarship has largely failed to see the *relevance* of Messiahship for a Jew like Paul. But part of the point of Messiahship, whether in the *Psalms of Solomon*, the Qumran texts, or even in his strange way Josephus, was that when the Messiah came he would be the ruler of the whole world. 'His dominion will be from the one sea to the other; from the River to the ends of the earth.'[8] Whether or not the Gentiles knew or cared that Israel's Messiah would be their rightful Lord, that is what many Jews believed. Paul, believing Jesus to be the Messiah, clearly shared that belief.

Second, it has often been assumed (a) that Messiahship is a 'political' category as well as, or even instead of, a 'religious' one; and (b) that Paul's message, and that of the early church in general, was by contrast 'religious' rather than 'political'. I shall say more about this in the next chapter, when it will become clear just how wrong-headed that false alternative is when applied to the first century, to say nothing for the moment about any other period including our own. In particular, within the Lutheran mindset that conditioned much of the exegetical spadework of the last two centuries, the 'two kingdoms' model dominated the horizon, forbidding access to layers of Paul's mind which only now are coming to light. Ironically, those who in our own day have decided that Paul was a 'political' thinker *rather than* a 'religious' or 'theological' one have, in maintaining that false either/or, perpetuated a particular theological point of view and thereby have ignored the role of Messiahship in Paul for the opposite reason. Such are the ironies of scholarship, and the backwaters into which they lure unsuspecting students.

Let us then return to the main flow of the river, both of Paul's thought and of our own exposition of it. I argued in the previous chapter that Paul belongs firmly on the map of that Jewish thought which was characterized by the dynamic interplay of creation and covenant. I have now argued that he believed Jesus to be Israel's Messiah, the one in whom God's purpose for Israel, and even (we dare say) God's purpose for himself, was fulfilled, and that he made that belief a central and major strand in his thinking and writing. I now want to propose that, in doing so, Paul drew heavily on what we can only call 'apocalyptic' categories, and that these, so far from undermining his theology of creation, covenant and Messiah, serve rather to contextualize them and give them specific focus.

3. Apocalyptic in Paul

It all depends, of course, what you mean by 'apocalyptic'. As I said earlier, the word 'apocalyptic' has been used in a great many ways over the last fifty or more years. Klaus Koch wrote a famous book about the agonized German attempts to get rid of apocalyptic after Schweitzer, and its rehabilitation by some later writers.[9] But the rehabilitation has in some cases been just as damaging as the elimination, because it has depended on a demonstrably false view of what second-Temple Jews, including Paul, believed about God's ultimate purposes for the world. There may no doubt have been some who did believe that one day God would abolish the space-time universe for ever, in a cosmic conflagration with no subsequent phoenix-like new world as in Stoicism. But such views are hard to demonstrate in second-Temple literature. The old contrast between 'prophecy' and 'apocalyptic', in which the former is about God's action within the present world and the latter is about the demolition of this world and the establishment of something totally different, never represented more than a glimmer of the truth. It might be truer to say that 'apocalyptic' (within the second-Temple Jewish tradition; I say nothing here about non-Jewish apocalyptic movements and writings, important though they are in their own way) represents what happens to prophecy under certain historical and theological circumstances, notably continued oppression and the puzzle of what God is going to do about it and how. In addition, of course, it represents a particular literary genre, with several important variations, designed to indicate by its *form* what it communicated by its *substance*, namely the 'revelation' or 'unveiling' of things otherwise kept secret. That, lexically, is of course what 'apocalyptic' means, and if we are to keep any handle on the word it would be useful to bear this in mind.

What has happened in the last generation of scholarship, however, is that the word 'apocalyptic' has been used as a shorthand to denote a specific way of thinking about God and the world, and a way of understanding Paul in particular. According to this way, the divine solution to the problems of the world is simply to break in to an otherwise unfruitful and corrupt ongoing historical process and to do something radically new. Over against any idea that God was quietly and steadily working his purposes out as year succeeded to year, this would-be 'apocalyptic' theology insists that, for Paul, God broke in to history, the history of Israel, the history of the world, in his action in Jesus and particularly in his cross; and God will do so again, very soon from Paul's perspective, in the second coming through which what God accomplished through Jesus will be brought to completion. In this kind of 'apocalyptic' we find the very opposite of a 'covenant' theology in which the age-old promises are to be fulfilled through the long unwinding of Israel's and the world's story. On the contrary: God is doing a new thing. Jesus bursts onto the scene in a shocking, unexpected, unimaginable fashion, the crucified Christ offered as a slap in the face to Israel and the world, folly to Gentiles and a scandal to Jews. The result is new creation, not so much *creatio ex vetere* but a fresh *creatio ex nihilo*. I intend by all this to sum up, and I hope not to caricature (despite necessary brevity), the influential work of J. Christian Beker on the one hand and J. Louis Martyn on the other, both drawing in different ways on one of my own heroes, the late Ernst Käsemann.[10]

But, like most of my heroes, Käsemann at this point had feet of clay – and indeed that image, borrowed as it is from Daniel 2, can serve as the beginning of an alternative account, again given briefly here with reference to my fuller accounts.[11] The book of Daniel is the Old Testament's best-known example both of the literary genre 'apocalyptic' and of the main feature of its contents, namely the revelation of secrets, of hidden mysteries. Apocalyptic depends upon a particular view of the world, namely the idea (which we already find, for instance, in Genesis and Deuteronomy) that the created order is divided into two, earth and heaven.[12] Within the twofold created universe, humans have the capacity to investigate things on earth; but only God, and perhaps other beings like angels, have the capacity to understand, and (should they so wish) to reveal to mortals, the things in heaven. Various devices are used for this revelation. It remains an open question how much the literary forms correspond to actual visions and religious experiences. People have dreams which are interpreted by another human being (as in Daniel 2) or by an angel (as in Daniel 7); they may have extended visions in which angels tell them things, as in parts of the book of Revelation; and so on. Thus apocalyptic characteristically speaks of the unveiling or revelation of mysteries, hidden secrets known in heaven but not before known on earth.

Among the mysteries which apocalyptic characteristically reveals, through whichever device, is *the plan of God*, sometimes in terms of lengthy accounts, actual or symbolic, of the history of the world or of Israel, usually reaching or about to reach a climax in the time when the book is being written. Sometimes it is simply secret mysteries about God, God's character and purpose, and so on. But as soon as we put it like this we ought to realize that we are describing something utterly central to Paul, even though he reports few visions (and is fairly reticent about those, too) and interprets no dreams. It is false to see Colossians and Ephesians, in this respect at least, as a step away from Paul's own rootedly Jewish context. When Paul declares in Colossians 2 that all the treasures of wisdom and knowledge are hidden in the Messiah, he is not invoking a non-Jewish idea of secret knowledge, but a fairly typical Jewish belief in mysteries which God always intended to reveal at the right time. This is how Paul's apostolic mission is described in Ephesians 3.8–11: that God gave him grace to bring to the Gentiles the news of the boundless riches of the Messiah, and to make all people see the plan of the mystery hidden for ages in God who created all things, namely that through the church the many-splendoured wisdom of God might be made known to the rulers and authorities in the heavenly places in accordance with the eternal purpose now carried out through the Messiah, Jesus. Granted, this is not the language of dream and interpretation we find in some of the classic apocalypses. The literary form has changed, but it has changed because of the realization, rather than the rejection, of the content. Paul believes that the ultimate dramatic apocalypse, the great unveiling of all God's mysteries, the full disclosure of God's secret plan, *has already come about* in and through the events concerning the Messiah, Jesus, particularly through his death and resurrection. Insofar as there is a correspondence in form between Paul's speaking or writing about this and the great apocalyptic books such as 4 Ezra or *2 Baruch*, it is as though the events concerning Jesus constitute the 'vision', and he is playing the part of the angel in explaining to the puzzled onlookers – in this case, the whole Gentile world – how these strange events actually unveil God's mysteries, and how the whole picture now works out.

In particular, of course, Paul is eager to explain in many passages the way in which God's long and many-staged plan of salvation has come to fruition. He eschews the 'four kingdoms' approach of Daniel 2 and 7, or the laboured recital of kings and battles in Daniel 10 and 11. Instead, we have, as in several second-Temple books of a broadly apocalyptic character, various retellings of the story of Israel from Abraham to the coming of the Messiah, and indeed beyond. I have already spoken of this in the previous chapter; this is one of those places where, once we understand how 'apocalyptic' works, the convergence between it and what I have called 'covenantal' thinking becomes apparent. One of the things which is 'unveiled' is precisely *how the covenant plan has been worked out*, how God has at last done what he said he would do, even though it doesn't look like what anyone had thought it would.

This brings us back again to Romans, where Paul uses the word *apokalypteō* itself, not that that would necessarily be anything other than a lexical coincidence. Exactly in line with what I said a moment ago vis-à-vis Colossians and Ephesians, Paul sees himself, writing Romans, as in one sense like the angel in an apocalypse, looking at the events of Jesus' death and resurrection and explaining what it is that is thereby revealed. 'In the gospel', he declares in Romans 1.17, 'God's righteousness is revealed,' *apokalyptetai*, from faith to faith. And by 'God's righteousness', as I argued in Chapter 2, he means not least 'God's faithfulness to the covenant plan, the plan through which the whole creation would be liberated from corruption, evil and death'. This is the point at which creation and covenant, Messiah and apocalyptic belong exactly together.

This leads us back once more to Romans 3, where Paul picks up the same theme. This time (3.21) he uses *pephanerōtai* rather than *apokalyptetai*, but the point is the same. Against the dark backdrop of the revelation (same word) of God's wrath, and the inclusion of all humanity within it so that even the Jews, the bearers of the saving purpose, had themselves become part of the problem, Paul declares that God's righteousness, God's saving covenant faithfulness, God's restorative justice, has been made manifest, disclosed, revealed. The secret truth about God and his purpose has been laid bare. This time the focus is on the way in which God has made full provision for the human sin which lies at the root of the problem: the sacrificial death of Jesus, in faithful obedience to God's saving plan, has provided the remedy. This opens the way for the quasi-apocalyptic retelling of the story of Israel from Abraham to the present in chapter 4, and more fully in chapters 9 and 10.

We thus arrive at the preliminary conclusion: for Paul, 'apocalyptic', the sudden, dramatic and shocking unveiling of secret truths, the sudden shining of bright heavenly light on a dark and unsuspecting world, is after all what God had always intended. One of the central tensions in Paul's thought, giving it again and again its creative edge, is the clash between the fact that God always intended what has in fact happened and the fact that not even the most devout Israelite had dreamed that it would happen like this. We cannot expound Paul's covenant theology in such a way as to make it a smooth, steady progress of historical fulfilment; but nor can we propose a kind of 'apocalyptic' view in which nothing that happened before Jesus is of any value even as preparation. In the messianic events of Jesus' death and resurrection Paul believes *both* that the covenant promises were at last fulfilled *and* that this constituted a massive and dramatic irruption into the processes of world history unlike anything before or since. And at the heart of both parts of this tension stands the cross of the Messiah, at once the long-awaited fulfilment and the slap in the face for all human pride. Unless we hold on to both parts of this truth we are missing something absolutely central to Paul.

Unlike anything before or since; but not quite unlike something yet to happen. Paul believed firmly that Jesus would come again as judge. There is no space here for a full review of the rich relevant material. But four things stand out which must be factored in to this treatment of messianic apocalypticism in Paul.

First, for Paul the language of 'coming' is at least potentially misleading. The word *parousia*, often rendered as 'coming' within Christian scholarship, actually means 'presence', as opposed to 'absence'. But, precisely within the implicit cosmology of 'apocalyptic' Judaism, heaven and earth are not after all separated by a great distance; they are certainly not different locations within the same spatial continuum. It is more appropriate to think of them as overlapping and interlocking dimensions, so that what matters is not Jesus' 'coming', as though from a great distance, but his 'personal presence', or indeed 'royal presence' since that is how *parousia* was often used in relation to the emperor or other monarchs. Colossians 3.4, like (interestingly) 1 John 3.2, uses the verb *phaneroō* to refer to this event: not 'when he arrives', but 'when he *appears*' – when he is unveiled, when, in the coming apocalyptic moment, the final secret of the world, already announced in the gospel, is made clear to all people, when every knee shall bow at his name. In that context Paul can even speak of the Christian church as already seated in the heavenly places in the Messiah, so that the church, too, will be revealed, unveiled. The present true life of the church has itself become one of the heavenly secrets to be manifest in the final apocalypse, precisely because the church is 'in the Messiah'. We shall examine all this in more detail in Chapter 7 below.

Second, the key passage in 1 Thessalonians 4, an 'apocalyptic' passage in Paul if ever there was one, should not be treated as though it predicted what in North America at the moment has become a major motif, namely the 'rapture' in which God's people will be caught up literally into mid-air, leaving homes, cars and family behind and escaping for ever the space-time world as it goes spinning off to its doom. The point of the passage is the comfort of the mourners. Paul's main aim is to insist that those who have died, and those who are still alive when the Messiah appears in his royal presence, will together inherit the new age which he will usher in. But the language which Paul uses to make the point, a combination of classic apocalyptic images, should be seen for what it is: an evocation of Daniel 7 (the son of man coming on the clouds) and of the revelation or apocalypse on Mount Sinai (the shout and the trumpet, and Moses coming down with the Law).

But, third, Paul has combined these themes with a very different one, without (so far as I can tell) any major precedent in biblical or second-Temple Jewish literature. The word *parousia* itself, and the language of 'meeting' which Paul uses in 1 Thessalonians 4.17, is not, like so many of his key terms, familiar from the Septuagint. It evokes the scene, familiar from much Hellenistic and Roman writing, of a king or emperor paying a state visit to a city or province. As he approaches, the citizens come out to meet him at some distance from the city, not in order then to hold a meeting out in the countryside, but to escort him into the city. 'Meeting the Lord in the air' is not a way of saying 'in order then to stay safely away from the wicked world'. It is the prelude to the implied triumphant return to earth where the Messiah will reign, and his people with him, as

Lord, saviour and judge. And in that context *parousia* means what it means in imperial rhetoric: the royal presence of the true Lord or emperor. This points on to the theme of the next chapter, since precisely in Thessalonians, as in Philippians and Romans, we find clear signs that Paul's gospel of Jesus the Messiah claims to be the reality of which Caesar's empire, with all its trappings, is simply a parody.

Fourth, there are some passages in Paul which are often taken to refer to this final apocalypse, but which Paul probably did not intend that way. When he speaks of God's wrath coming 'at last' upon the inhabitants of Judaea (1 Thessalonians 2.16) he is probably not thinking of the great moment he describes in chapter 4, but of an interim judgment, warned of by Jesus himself, on the city and the people that had rejected their Messiah. Indeed, when he grieves over his fellow Jews in Romans 9—11, I think part at least of that grief is conditioned by his awareness that they are living under the shadow of impending national disaster. Likewise, when he writes in 2 Thessalonians that the young church should not be worried if they get a letter saying that the Day of the Lord had arrived, it is clear that he cannot be referring to anything of the same order as the renewal of creation in Romans 8 or the royal presence of the Lord in 1 Thessalonians 4 or 1 Corinthians 15 – still less to the end of the space-time universe, which the Thessalonians themselves would presumably have noticed. Here again I think Paul is aware – and his allusions to what we know as Matthew 24 and parallels may bear this out – that early tradition included solemn warnings from Jesus himself about the imminent destruction of Jerusalem and the Temple. This is the event which had to happen within a generation; and this, I think – though this is bound to be controversial – is why Paul felt a sense of urgency in his mission to the Gentile world, which has commonly been thought of as a feature of his apocalyptic-style theology. It was not that he had to save as many people as he could, a quick representative sample, before the ultimate end of all things. It was that he had to plant stable Jew-plus-Gentile churches on Gentile soil before the event occurred which would make Jews blame the Christians for letting the side down, and which would invite Gentiles to sneer at Jews for having lost their home and capital city. Here as elsewhere, when we understand Paul's apocalyptic theology we will find it rooted within, and referring to, actual historical events.

Paul, then, held what we might call a covenantal and apocalyptic theology in which, in surprising fulfilment of the covenant, God had unveiled his plan, his character, and not least his saving, restorative justice through the events concerning Jesus the Messiah, and would complete this revelation once for all at Jesus' final appearing, his eventual royal presence. And this means, as is well known, that his theology has the character of *inaugurated eschatology*, that is, of a sense that God's ultimate future has come forwards into the middle of history, so that the church is living within – indeed, is constituted precisely by living simultaneously within! – God's new world and the present one. The age to come has already arrived with Jesus; but it will be consummated in the future. The church must order its life and witness, its holiness and love, along that axis.

There is one final implication of this to which I draw attention in concluding this chapter, an implication which I shall spell out more fully later on (so that this mention, in anticipating something yet to come more fully, deliberately embodies the principle I am expounding). It concerns justification by faith. Surprisingly, a good deal of the discussion of this central theme, not least in the literature reacting unfavourably to the so-called 'new perspective', seems to have downplayed the context of covenant and apocalyptic, of inaugurated eschatology, within which Paul himself locates it, most obviously in Romans 3. The point is this: God's full and final revelation of his restorative justice, his plan to put the whole world to rights, is what will occur at the end, with the royal presence of Jesus as judge and saviour. But this restorative justice, this covenant faithfulness through which creation itself will be redeemed, has been unveiled already, in advance, in the apocalyptic events of Jesus' messianic death and resurrection. Precisely in those events, as they are portrayed in the 'gospel', the royal announcement made by Jesus' apostolic heralds, God has declared in advance that he has dealt with sin and death, and has summoned the world to the obedience of faith, with the corollary that all those who believe find themselves declared in advance, as part of the apocalyptic unveiling of the ultimate future, to be within God's true family, whether they be Jew or Gentile. The whole point about 'justification by faith' is that it is something which happens *in the present time* (Romans 3.26) as a proper anticipation of the eventual judgment which will be announced, on the basis of the whole life led, in the future (Romans 2.1–16). Until justification is set firmly within this eschatological, as well as covenantal and apocalyptic, framework, we shall never be able to understand what Paul is talking about. And here, too, we find his thought coming back to rest on the point at which we began, the point where covenant, Messiahship and apocalyptic meet, the point which Paul determined to hold on to as the still centre of his whirling thoughts when he arrived at Corinth: Jesus the Messiah, and him crucified.

When we thus tie together the multi-coloured threads of Paul's theology, and place them within not only the Jewish but also the Hellenistic and Roman worlds in which he lived, we ought to be struck (though many have not been!) by a world of meaning which would have been obvious, second nature we might say, to Paul and his hearers. By hailing Jesus as king, as son of God, as the world's true Lord; by declaring that with his coming God's new age had begun, so that the 'good news' of his accession to world sovereignty must ring out round the world; by announcing that one day his 'royal presence' would appear and call everyone to celebration and to account; and by insisting that through this Jesus were to be found salvation, justice and peace – in all these ways and more, Paul was saying that Jesus was Lord, and that Caesar was not. His theology of creation and covenant, of Messiahship and apocalyptic, thus projects us forwards into the topic of the next chapter: gospel and empire.

are inclined to oppose all governments and structures of authority, and the further right you go the more you are inclined to support firm and stable government and civic authority. Since we come equipped with this sliding scale, it has been normal for readers of Paul to glance at Romans 13 and assume that Paul's emphatic insistence on obedience to the ruling authorities places him at least in a centre-right position on our spectrum. But of course Paul doesn't belong on our spectrum. He belongs, if anywhere, on the map of political opinion formed by the peculiar circumstances of second-Temple Judaism, shaped by factors very different from those in Europe and America in the eighteenth and subsequent centuries.

Second, we must recognize that the modern western separation of theology and society, religion and politics, would have made no sense either to Paul or to any of his contemporaries, whether Jewish, Greek or Roman. Israel believed that its God was the creator, ruler and judge of the whole world. The gods of the Greco-Roman world were woven into the fabric of social and civic life; the newest god in the pantheon, Caesar himself, was a living example of the uniting of the divine and human spheres. Most biblical scholarship, both so-called conservative and so-called liberal, has projected our modern categories back on to the New Testament, when in fact a glance even at the sixteenth and seventeenth centuries, to look no further back, would reveal just how anachronistic our assumptions really are.

Third, a word about how we detect the presence of allusion and echo behind explicit statements. This is one of those points where exegesis is having to take account of larger patterns and narratives than had emerged from earlier scholarship. An example from a very different sphere: Graham Robb, in his remarkable book *Strangers*, tracks the way in which, in an entire transnational culture, writers were able to allude to homosexual affection and practice through the use of key words, names, colours and images, at a time when such things could not be published openly.[1] I came upon another example in the course of writing the lectures on which this book is based: during the Chinese cultural revolution, a playwright was attacked because, in writing historical plays about a period several hundreds of years earlier, he had (like Shakespeare, in fact) launched coded critiques of the present regime which only those in the know could pick up – but which had in fact been picked up, and he was prosecuted. In the first century, exactly the same has been argued in relation to Philo on the one hand and Nero on the other.[2]

In the New Testament itself, the best-known work on the detection of allusion and echo is that of Richard Hays, in his famous *Echoes of Scripture in the Letters of Paul.*[3] He offers seven criteria which, were this a whole course instead of a single lecture, we could profitably apply to 'echoes of Caesar' alongside 'echoes of scripture':

1. Availability: was the material readily available and knowable in the culture at the time?

2. Volume: is the word, or the syntactical pattern, repeated sufficiently in the immediate context to establish an 'audible' volume? How significant is this material in the original source, and in its appropriation elsewhere in Paul's day?

3. Recurrence: does the word or theme recur elsewhere in the Pauline corpus, sufficient for us to be able to establish a broader base of meaning?

4. Thematic coherence: does the theme cohere well with other aspects of what Paul is saying? How well does it sit with the rest of the train of thought of the passage and the letter? (This is the point at which, of course, any attempt to detect 'echoes of Caesar' in Paul will run up against the question: what then do you say about Romans 13?)

5. Historical plausibility: could Paul have intended this meaning, or is it anachronistic or out of context when we predicate it of him? (We note, as an aside, that the charge of anachronism hangs over the head of all exegesis guilty of the religion/politics split I mentioned a moment ago.) Would Paul's readers have understood what he was hinting at? Does the intertextuality of the wider culture, the web of allusion and echo familiar in the world at large, allow, facilitate or encourage this kind of an implicit storyline?

6. History of interpretation: have other interpreters from other ages read the text in any way like this? (Again, an aside: if the answer were always 'yes', exegetes would be out of a job, since biblical study would collapse into church history; but the fact that exegetes have often been more concerned to apply the text to their own times than to understand it within its own mean that the answer 'no' will not be particularly surprising, and certainly ought not to be taken to mean, without more ado, that something has gone wrong.)

7. Satisfaction: does this reading enable the text to speak with new coherence and clarity? Does the text, read this way, settle down and make itself at home? Is there, in Hays's word, an 'aha' of fresh understanding when we read it like this?

These seven criteria are obviously not exhaustive, and apply at different levels and in different ways.[4] Like everything in history and literature, they regularly include what used to be dismissed as subjective judgments, but are none the worse for that; after all, the implicit theories with which they compete are themselves no less subjective. We perhaps need to comment that, though this seems complex and cumbersome, it is only so for us, not for the first-century writers and readers we are attempting to understand. If, two thousand years from now, a historian were attempting to understand the writings of our world, he or she would need to work back, with labour and difficulty, into a universe of discourse where minor characters from soap operas jostled with small-time politicians, alluding to weapons inspectors on the one hand and to boat races on the other, where an echo of Shakespeare might not be recognized though a line from an Elton John song probably would. We move effortlessly in this world, but others would have to reconstruct it inch by inch. That is the kind of thing we are trying to do, with very limited information, with Paul and his world. The one thing we can be sure of is that it was more complex and many-layered than most of our attempts at reconstruction can ever be.

So much for brief introductory remarks. I shall now set out some key features of the early Roman empire and its ideology and cult. Then I shall glance at the standard Jewish critiques of pagan empire, which formed the world of thought from which Paul came. Then I shall turn to the key texts to construct my substantial argument. As we shall see, precisely the categories we have already studied, creation and covenant, Messiah and apocalyptic, project Paul forwards into confrontation with the main earthly power of his day.

2. Caesar's Empire and Its Ideology

When Paul was converted, the Roman empire as such was two generations old. The ancient and venerable Roman Republic had collapsed into civil war following the murder of Julius Caesar. Several years of bloody and divisive conflict had eventually led to the emergence of Octavian, Caesar's adopted heir, who took the title Augustus and reigned supreme over Rome and its burgeoning empire for the last two decades BC and the first fourteen years AD. His adopted heir Tiberius carried on and consolidated his work, being followed by the disastrous Gaius Caligula and the shrewd but weak Claudius. Claudius' death in AD 54 left the way clear for Nero, who came to the throne in a blaze of optimism as a bright new hope, and left it, mourned by some, loathed by many, in 68, precipitating the so-called 'year of the four emperors', a few brief months of total chaos ended by Vespasian establishing a new dynasty. During this period the empire stretched right around the Mediterranean world and some distance into much of the hinterland. Having seen off its main rival, Carthage, some centuries before, Rome sat in luxury at the middle of a web of power, influence and money.

Within this historical framework, the ideology of empire rested on the transference to it of the old ideals of the Republic. Cicero had argued, a century before Paul, that Rome and its people were the natural home of freedom. They had established a democracy, the pretence of which was kept up throughout the early imperial period. So strong was Cicero's belief in Rome's freedom, and the responsibility to share this with the rest of the world, that when his political enemies had him banished and pulled his house down, his friends put up, on its site, a statue of the goddess Liberty. Similarly, the Republic had long prided itself on its justice, and in the middle years of Augustus' reign 'Iustitia', too, became an official goddess: Rome possessed Justice, and had an obligation to share it with the rest of the world. Augustus was hailed, following the civil war, as the bringer of peace – though cynics might comment that peace came from military exhaustion rather than virtue, and one Roman cynic did put into the mouth of a conquered foe, a century later, the accusation that the Romans created a wilderness and labelled it 'peace'. Augustus was also hailed as 'Saviour', in gratitude for rescuing Rome from civil strife and external enemies. Freedom, justice, peace and salvation were the imperial themes that you could expect to meet in the mass media of the ancient world, that is, on statues, on coins, in poetry and song and speeches. And the announcement of these themes, focused of course on the person of the emperor who accomplished and guaranteed them, could be spoken of as *euangelion*, 'good news', 'gospel'.[5]

The poets and historians, too, were busy telling a new story. Virgil, Horace, Livy and others in their different ways produced a new grand narrative of empire, a long eschatology which had now reached its climax. (Cicero had tried to do the same, of course, congratulating Rome, somewhat prematurely, on coming to new birth at the time of his consulship.) The Augustan court poets told how Rome had come through a long apprenticeship, a period of preparation, and now at last was in her rightful place as mistress of the world. This ideology, like most imperial rhetoric, got rewritten as the empire wore on, but managed to survive the ridiculous chaos of AD 69 and carry on well into subsequent centuries. And the symbols of empire were everywhere apparent. Rome's ruthless and efficient military machine swept all before it – well, almost all, allowing for the odd disaster like the loss of legions in Germany. Rebellions were punished with cold brutality, making the cross an effective and feared symbol of imperial might long before it came to symbolize anything else. Rome's system of justice – which, to be fair, was often a considerable improvement on the local systems over which it superimposed itself – supplied tribunals and courts of law answerable, ultimately, to the emperor himself. Roman provincial governors could be, and sometimes were, put on trial at the end of their terms of office if the locals complained of mismanagement. Rome levied taxes, of course, ostensibly to pay for all these privileges of freedom and justice, but also to increase the magnificence of the mother city. The royal family, both the emperor himself and his predecessors, and his wife and children, were well known through statues and coins. From Spain to Syria, everybody knew about Rome, what it stood for, what it did, and who was in charge of it.

Within this framework of imperial ideology, the emperor-cult itself was the fastest-growing religion in Paul's world, that of the eastern Mediterranean. Augustus had consolidated his own position by declaring that Julius Caesar, his adopted father, had been divinized after his murder; most subsequent emperors paid their predecessors the same compliment, often with the convenient fiction of getting someone to testify that they had seen the late ruler's soul ascending to heaven. The new emperor would then claim the title 'son of god', even though in most cases the sonship was adoptive.

Most of the early emperors were careful not to claim divine honours in Rome itself. 'Son of god' was quite sufficient. But in the

East, where rulers and monarchs had long been regarded as divine, there was not only no problem but a strong pressure to establish the emperor-cult, not least because special rewards were available for cities that did so. The centre of Ephesus was rebuilt to highlight the imperial temple. The new imperial temple in Corinth was built on a plinth at the western end of the forum, deliberately higher than all the previous temples in the area. Games, festivals and celebrations of various sorts were organized in honour of the emperor; priesthoods were established; statues of the emperor and his family were constructed which borrowed motifs from the mainstream Greco-Roman pantheon. As far as most of the Roman world was concerned, the 'divinity' of the emperor was obvious and uncontroversial. He and his troops had, after all, conquered the known world; they obviously possessed a power greater than anyone else's.

This was the world within which Paul went about declaring the 'gospel' according to which Jesus of Nazareth, crucified by Roman soldiers, had been raised from the dead and was the world's true Lord, claiming universal allegiance. But Paul was not working this out in a vacuum. He was drawing on several Jewish traditions which, he believed, had come to a climax with Jesus. We must now look briefly at these, before turning to his own writings.

3. Jewish Critique of Pagan Empire

By Paul's day the Jewish people had had plenty of experience of living under pagan empire. Apart from the brief time of independent monarchy under David and Solomon, most of their formative years had been spent either as slaves in Egypt (or at least as telling the story of being slaves in Egypt) or as exiles in Babylon (or telling the story of being exiled there). Even during the periods of independence the threat of foreign powers was never far away.

The central Jewish account of how to live under such circumstances was hammered out by the prophets. Samuel told the people in no uncertain terms about how pagan rulers behave and warned them that a king of their own would probably do the same.[6] Amos inveighed against pagan rulers before turning his critique on Israel and Judah themselves. Isaiah declared that the true God was using Assyria's power for his own purposes, to punish his people, but that Assyria herself would then be punished in turn.[7] The rise of Babylon was marked by oracles predicting its eventual destruction,[8] and though Jeremiah saw it as the necessary instrument of God's wrath against Judah, his final depiction of Babylon's overthrow is more devastating still.[9] In particular, the central section of Isaiah, chapters 40—55, contains a massive and mocking denunciation of pagan religion and the imperial power it sustains, while simultaneously declaring that the one true God had called Cyrus, a Persian who didn't even know this God, to perform his will in setting the exiles free from Babylon – and while also unveiling, slowly and mysteriously, the redeeming work of the figure called YHWH's Servant. A not dissimilar theology is found in narrative form in the book of Esther. Finally, we note the book of Daniel, which scorns the power and religious pretension of pagan empire and exalts the Jewish heroes who resist it. Daniel is of course the book in which we find the influential narrative in which four pagan kingdoms arise in sequence, the last one being overthrown when God establishes his kingdom and vindicates his people.[10]

Things are not straightforward, by our Procrustean standards, in any of these books. When God acts to rescue the three righteous Jews from the furnace, or Daniel from the den of lions, they are then given top jobs in the imperial civil service. Jeremiah tells the exiles to settle down and seek Babylon's welfare as long as they live there.[11] At points like these we realize how inadequate our left–right spectrum is for understanding how the Jewish people thought about earthly rulers. Radical subversion of pagan political systems does not mean support for anarchy. The Jewish political belief we find in books like this was based on a strong theology of creation, fall and providence: the one God had in fact created all the world, including all rulers, and though they were often exceedingly wicked God was overruling their whims for his own strange and often hidden purposes, and would judge them in their turn. This meant that a classic Jewish position, which echoes on well into the Christianity of the second and third centuries, seems to us today to play from both ends of the spectrum at once. The rulers are wicked and will be judged, especially when they persecute God's people. But God wants the world to be ruled, rather than to descend into anarchy and chaos, and his people must learn to live under pagan rule even though it means constant vigilance against compromise with paganism itself.

We can watch this biblical inheritance being retrieved in various second-Temple texts, not to mention movements, within Paul's own period. The Wisdom of Solomon, written perhaps not many years before Paul's letters, declares that it will teach the rulers of the world how to behave. It opens with the dramatic scene where the wicked rulers persecute the righteous, and declare that, once they have killed them, they will be gone for good. No, they won't, says Wisdom, drawing on Daniel 12: they will be back, there will be a judgment, and the wicked rulers will be horrified to learn their own fate. Therefore, declares the writer, you rulers had better beware: there is a God who will summon you to judgment. What you need, like Solomon, is Wisdom itself, so that you can order yourselves and your responsibilities aright. The second half of the book is a remarkable retelling of the early part of the Old Testament, focusing particularly, and significantly, on God's overthrow of Pharaoh and rescue of Israel. This story was not told, we may be sure, for purely antiquarian interest. What God did for Israel before, what God did to the pagan king before, God could and would do again.

The critique of pagan empire, and the promise of its overthrow, comes into strident expression in some of the Qumran texts, an obvious example being the War Scroll, 1QM. There, imagery from the Psalms and prophets is reused to say, in no uncertain terms, that God will act decisively, that a ceremonial and solemn holy war will be undertaken, and that the nations will be ground to powder under the feet of the righteous Jews. God, with his justice and holiness, will win the absolute victory. At the same time, we know that at various stages the members of the sect were still hoping to influence the Jerusalem priesthood (as in for instance 4QMMT) and seize power. Had they done so they might have found themselves precipitated into the more complex, less black-and-white world of many of their contemporaries. We note, for example, the very different viewpoints of the various books of the Maccabees. Thus, though from time to time we hear in Paul echoes from 1QM and similar texts (notably, for instance, in 2 Thessalonians, causing some to doubt its authenticity), they are combined with other themes for which the Qumran writers had less use.

Several first-century writers drew on Daniel and similar traditions to construct apocalyptic works, such as 4 Ezra and *2 Baruch*, in which Daniel's critique of pagan empire, not least his sequence of four wicked kingdoms rising up and being overthrown, was reapplied to the writers' own day. These texts are responding to the fall of Jerusalem in AD 70, and are reusing traditional material both to lament, to understand what had happened (maybe, somehow, they muse, this was all a necessary punishment, like the Babylonian exile itself), and to promise a future vindication. A different configuration of traditional images and themes, brought about by a different historical situation. We may contrast this with Josephus' strikingly different re-reading of the same texts: scripture, he says, predicted that at that period a world ruler would indeed arise from Judaea, but this referred not to a Jewish Messiah but to Vespasian, who went from Jerusalem to Rome to become emperor (and whose dynasty was, of course, supplying Josephus with his state pension as he wrote). But even Josephus still belongs on the Jewish map, since he could claim with some justice to be applying, albeit in a radically new way, the ancient doctrine of God's providence working through pagan rulers to punish his people (Josephus blames the radical revolutionaries, of course) and rule the world. On this map, too, a full picture would have to plot the explosive set of variations played on this theme by a young Jewish prophet in the reign of Tiberius who announced that God was at last becoming King, who went to his death in the belief that this would somehow bring about that long-awaited reign, and whose followers declared that he had been raised from the dead. The connections between the thought, and particularly the actions, of Jesus of Nazareth and the developed theology of Paul form, of course, an entire topic in themselves, to which we shall return briefly in our closing chapter.

This is the map, or at least part of the map, of first-century Jewish attitudes towards pagan authority. It amounts to a theology of earthly rulers quite different from that assumed by most western Christians today, but it is a theology which grows exactly out of the picture of creation and covenant I sketched in the second chapter. God wants the world to be ordered, to keep evil in check, otherwise wickedness simply flourishes and naked power and aggression wins. But the rulers of the world are themselves answerable to God, not least at the point where they use their power to become just like the bullies they are supposed to be restraining. Meanwhile, God is working out a very different purpose, which will result in the vindication of his people and the judgment of the Pharaohs and Babylons of the world.

All this is based, of course, on a creational monotheism which, faced with evil in the world, declares that God will one day put it all to rights, and that we can see advance signs of that in systems of justice and government even when they are imperfect. This leaves no room for a dualism in which pagan rulers are thoroughly bad and can be ignored, or overthrown without thought for what will come next. Nor does it allow that kind of pantheism in which rulers are simply part of the fabric of the divinely ordered world, requiring unquestioning submission to their every whim. It would be fascinating to trace the ways in which, in European theology over the last few hundred years, these options have been tried and found wanting. But my lack of competence in that field is nicely sheltered behind my lack of space in this chapter, and I must now turn, none too soon, to the task of placing Paul on this map of Jewish critique of pagan empire.

4. Paul's Counter-Imperial Theology

We take a run at this theme from those we have studied in the previous two chapters. According to Paul's view of creation, the one God was responsible for the whole world and would one day put it to rights. According to his covenant theology, this God would rescue his people from pagan oppression. His messianic theology hailed Jesus as King, Lord and Saviour, the one at whose name every knee would bow. His apocalyptic theology saw God unveiling his own saving justice in the death and resurrection of the Messiah. At every point, therefore, we should expect what we in fact find: that, for Paul, Jesus is Lord and Caesar is not. We first sketch an outline of how this works, before turning to the key texts.

First, if Jesus is Israel's Messiah then he is the world's true Lord. This is the clear meaning both of several of the messianic biblical texts on which Paul drew and of their appropriation by other Jews of his day. For Paul, Jesus' messianic status and his world rulership was based on the fact of his resurrection. As in the Wisdom of Solomon, it is the defeat of death, the return of the martyred righteous, that signals to the earthly rulers that their game is up. If we wanted to cash this out theologically a bit further, we might suggest that, since earthly rulers have death as their ultimate weapon, the defeat of death in the resurrection is the overthrow of the ultimate enemy which stands behind all tyranny. That, I think, is part of the point of 1 Corinthians 15.20–28 and Colossians 2.14–15. But resurrection is more than defeat of an enemy. It is the inauguration of God's new world, the new creation which has already begun to take over the present creation with the unstoppable power of the creator God. The resurrection of the crucified Messiah thus functions in Paul's thought both as history, as theology, and (not least) as symbol, the symbol of a power which upstages anything military power can do.

Paul thus had fresh reason to articulate an essentially Jewish political theology, in line with that of the prophets. This involved not only a radical critique of pagan power, which as we shall see was focused especially on Rome as the obvious target in his own day, but also a radical restatement of the duty of God's people when living under present pagan rule. Not only in Romans 13, but in Colossians 1 and (if it is even an echo of Paul's voice) 1 Timothy 2, Paul declares that the powers in earth and heaven are the creation of the one God, and that it is right that they be obeyed. The manner of that obedience is instructive. Whatever we think of the historicity of Acts, the portrait of Paul before the authorities both pagan and Jewish tells us a good deal about the way in which the Jewish traditions were being reanimated and retrieved. He is prepared to submit to the courts, but is also more than prepared to remind them of their business and to call them to account when they overstep their duty. He uses his own Roman citizenship when it suits the demands of his mission. But at the same time he is fearless in announcing, and living by, a different allegiance. When the Paul of Acts is on trial in 17.7 for overthrowing the laws of Caesar by saying that there is 'another king, namely Jesus', we see what I take to be an authentic memory of the typical impression made by his gospel preaching.

It would be possible from here to explore the relevant material by means of key words and ideas: *Kyrios*, *Sōter*, *parousia*, *euangelion*, *dikaiosynē*, and so on. At each point we would find that the material (to return to Richard Hays's categories) was available, loud in volume, frequent in recurrence and thematic coherence, historically plausible, and, though routinely not noticed within much of the history of interpretation, enormously productive of that 'aha' which is one of the results of good historical exegesis. But I prefer to go straight for the main passages in question, and I start with a book I have so far, surprisingly, hardly mentioned, namely Philippians.

The closing verses of Philippians 3 (vv. 20–21) are one of the most obvious points at which to begin. Our citizenship, declares Paul, is in heaven, and it is from there that we await the Saviour, the Lord, Jesus the Messiah, who will change the body of our humiliation to be like the body of his glory, according to the power which gives him the ability to bring everything into subjection to himself. We do not have to suppose that everybody in Philippi was a Roman citizen (only a minority of them were, in fact), nor that everyone had taken a university course in current political rhetoric, to claim that this material corresponded closely to readily available and knowable imperial themes in the culture of the day. In claiming the citizenship of heaven, by contrast to the pretensions and corruptions of earth (vv. 17–19), Paul was drawing on a standard Jewish theme which we see in, for instance, Daniel, where the true God is referred to as, among other things, 'the God of heaven', the one who is sovereign over the kingdoms of mortals. This gives substance to the claim that Jesus is currently *in* heaven; this does not mean that he has gone into a sphere of no further interest to earth, but precisely that he is the one to whom sovereignty over the earth has been given. And this sovereignty is expressed in the classic Caesar-titles, 'saviour' and 'lord', backed up by Jesus' status as Messiah.[12] And, as in Psalm 57.3–5, God will send from on high to rescue his own from the spears, arrows and swords of the enemy; the God who is exalted over the heavens will extend his glory over the earth as well. And he will do this because, in fulfilment of Psalms 8 and 110, all things are subjected to Jesus both as the true Messiah and as the truly human being. The theme of God's power at work in Jesus connects very closely, of course, with that of the resurrection, as in Romans 1.3–4, Ephesians 1.19–22 and 1 Corinthians 15.27. Here in Philippians 3 it is invoked to say that what God did for Jesus in his resurrection, transforming his humiliated body into a glorious one, now incapable of suffering and death, God will do for all his people when he returns to reign on the transformed earth.

This sudden flourish of imperial language applied to Jesus at the end of Philippians 3 suggests, as I have argued elsewhere, a fresh reading of the whole chapter.[13] The key question is, what does Paul mean in verse 17 when he summons the Philippians to 'imitate him'? Up until that point he has been speaking of his own strange pilgrimage, from his pre-Christian celebration of the badges of his Jewish identity, through his sharing of the Messiah's death and resurrection and his discovery that in the Messiah he had all the true marks of God's covenant people, not least the suffering and the promise of resurrection which marked out the martyrs in particular. This is, it seems, what he was asking the Philippians to imitate.

But how could they? They were not Pharisees; they were not even Jewish. They had never celebrated their status as God's chosen people in the way that Paul had. No: but they were part of one of the proudest outposts of Roman civilization in the Greek world. Philippi had been a colony for about a century, and though many of the original local families would still have resented the Roman intrusion, the benefits that accrued to the whole community from its close ties with Rome and its power would be well known. In particular, they knew that if they were ever in difficulties, they could call on the emperor to come from the mother city and rescue them, because as saviour and lord he had the power to impose his will on the whole known world. My proposal is that Philippians 3, though important in its own right as a statement of how Paul understood his own pilgrimage, constitutes an example which Paul is holding out to them, an example of how they, too, must hear the call of God in Jesus to sit light to their civic status and be prepared to hail Jesus, not Caesar, as lord.

This is powerfully undergirded, of course, by Philippians 2.5–11, which has strong and detailed links with many parts of Philippians 3. I still hold the view that Paul wrote this poem himself, quite possibly for use at this point in this letter, and he certainly used it here in a way that integrates closely with the thrust of the letter as a whole. I draw on the work of Peter Oakes, who in his book on Philippians has teased out not only the many verbal connections between the poem and the imperial ideology, but also the parallel between the overall narrative of the poem and the regular rhetoric in which Caesar's rule was legitimated.[14] Caesar has been a servant of the state, by winning military victories, by putting up money for public works, and so on; we therefore hail him as lord, and entrust ourselves to him as our saviour. There are a great many points which could be developed here, but we simply note four.

First, Paul is drawing on Isaiah 40—55 (compare, for instance, 45.23 and 49.7), one of the classic passages of biblical critique of pagan empire as well as one of the most resounding and robust statements of Jewish monotheism.

Second, within this very monotheism Paul is locating Jesus, in a manner which once more demands a fully trinitarian explanation although Paul never gets round to providing one explicitly. The name which Jesus is given is the name *kyrios* – which is of course a title, not a name, but Paul means what he says, because here as elsewhere he is very conscious that in the LXX *kyrios* translates YHWH.[15] This is particularly important because the tendency has been in the last ten years to emphasize Paul's political critique at the expense of his Jewish roots on the one hand and his high Christology on the other, whereas with Paul you get all or nothing. Here again late western thought has imposed its false either/or – either serious Christian theology or radical political critique, but surely not both! – on the material, presumably out of a sense, understandable in the twentieth century but incomprehensible in the first, second or third, that orthodox theology sustains quiescent social and political life.

Third, the focus of the poem (the line in the middle which stands by itself in terms of the clear pattern of the other stanzas) is on 'the death of the cross'. We are here witnessing the rebirth of a symbol. The cross, as I said before, was already a powerful symbol in the ancient world. It spoke both of politics (the unstoppable military might of Rome) and of theology (the divinity of Caesar, whose power stood behind that of his armies). The early Christian use of the cross as a symbol was not simply a creation out of nothing. It took genius to see that the symbol which had spoken of Caesar's naked might now spoke of God's naked love. And I think that the genius in question belonged to Paul.

Fourth, this perspective on Philippians 2.5–11 enables us to give a different reading to verse 12, which has often puzzled interpreters who assume that whenever Paul mentions the word 'work' he is talking about justification. 'Therefore, my beloved family,' says Paul, 'work out your own salvation with fear and trembling.' He is not at all talking about the performance of moral good works designed to earn ultimate salvation. He knows that the Philippians live in a world where something called 'salvation' is on offer – at a price: where they are being invited to enjoy this salvation and live by its rules and submit to its lord. He is urging them to recognize that, as they have a different lord, so they have a very different salvation, and they must, with fear and trembling, work out in practice what it means to live by this salvation rather than the one their culture is forcing upon them.

There is much more that could be said about Philippians, but I want to move on westwards in northern Greece to Thessalonica. We looked in the previous chapter at the way in which Paul developed his multidimensional picture of Jesus' return, partly on the basis of Old Testament images about the appearance and judgment of God and partly, not least through the words *parousia* and *apantēsis*, on the basis of normal language about the royal arrival, appearance and presence of the emperor. What matters, again and again – and Philippians 3.20–21 is another example of this, even though the words *parousia* and so on do not occur – is the appearance of Jesus, rather than that of Caesar. In case anyone might think this far-fetched as an exegesis of 1 Thessalonians 4, confirmatory evidence is found in chapter 5, answering to Hays's criterion of 'volume'. Paul affirms, with gospel tradition behind him, that the day of the Lord will come like a thief in the night; for when (v. 3) people say 'peace and security', then sudden destruction will come upon them as on a woman in travail, and there will be no escape. Here, as often, Paul mixes his metaphors with relish: the coming of the thief in the night will mean that the woman will go into labour, therefore you mustn't get drunk, but must stay awake and put on your armour. But at the centre of it is the tell-tale phrase 'peace and security'. Once again we are in the homeland of imperial rhetoric. There are many occurrences of this phrase and others like it as the standard thing which Rome offered to its subject peoples. Come with us, obey the rule of Caesar, and we will look after you; 'peace and security' is in fact almost a definition of the Romans' *sōtēria*, salvation. It functions as a kind of global protection racket. And Paul mocks it. It's a hollow sham. What's more, at the very moment when they make the claim most strongly, then the destruction will come. Had he lived to witness what we call 'the year of the four emperors' he would undoubtedly have said, 'I told you so'. What he would have said at the rise of the Flavian dynasty is another question for another time.

I wish I could claim, while we are in the Thessalonian correspondence, that with this key I have unlocked the mysteries of the second chapter of the second letter, but I cannot. I cherish the hope that further work will enable us to understand in proper historical context 'the rebellion', 'the man of lawlessness', and 'the restrainer'. I would be happy to think that 'the man of lawlessness' was the emperor Gaius Caligula, trying to put up his statue in the Temple in Jerusalem, but without serious chronological revision of Paul's ministry this cannot be made to work. It is possible, however, that Paul has Caligula and his failed attempt in the back of his mind, and that he is guessing that another emperor might try the same trick again. If 2 Thessalonians were written under Nero, this might just fit. But this, as I say, leaves me both in the frustration of a loose end I cannot presently tie up and the excitement of more work waiting to be done.

From Thessalonica we come down through Greece to Corinth. Corinth in Paul's period prided itself on being, if anything, more Roman than Rome. I have already highlighted the way in which, in 1 Corinthians 15, Paul describes the resurrection of Jesus as inaugurating that period of history which is characterized by the sovereign rule of Jesus which will end with the destruction of all enemies, putting all things under his feet – echoing the same psalms to which Paul alludes in Philippians 3.21. We have noted, as well, the fact that in chapter 2 of the same letter Paul insists that the rulers of this age did not understand the wisdom of God which was hidden in Jesus, because if they had they would not have crucified him. Paul leaves this reference cryptic, but it does seem to belong closely with Colossians 2, as already noted. And the critique of the powers in Colossians points us across to Galatians 4, where the incarnation and death of Jesus, and the gift of the Spirit, spell the end of the rule of the *stoicheia*, the tutelary deities of the nations.

In this context, it is just possible that Bruce Winter's fascinating suggestion about Galatians may work.[16] According to Winter, at least one of the problems behind the situation in Galatia was the question of whether Christianity counted as a form of Judaism. If so, would they (like mainstream Jews) have been automatically exempted from taking part in the imperial cult? Or, if Christianity was regarded as a new sort of movement altogether, would the Christians be forced, like everyone else, to pay formal and religious homage to Caesar, as with Polycarp in Smyrna a century or so later? Interestingly, according to Acts, a senior Roman official in Corinth had given it as his verdict that the Christians were indeed a sort of Judaism, which meant that Christianity could spread in southern Greece without running the gauntlet of official persecution for failing to worship the emperor.[17] But without such a ruling in central Turkey the question was open, and controversial. The local Jewish community would not have wanted to see the Christians share, let alone take over, their exempt status. More importantly, one of the reasons the 'agitators' may have been persuading the Christians to get circumcised may not so much have been that they wanted them 'to do good works to earn their justification', but that they wanted to put on a good face, the good face of being fully paid-up Jews, before suspicious local officials wondering why they didn't join in with the imperial festivities and cult. I am not completely convinced by this theory, but it has a nagging historical rootedness about it, and I suspect that until something like this has been said the full story of Galatians may not yet have been told. This might perhaps have had something to do with Paul's warnings about 'another gospel'.

I pass over Ephesians with the merest mention. I have already spoken of the unveiling of God's power in the first chapter, and of the way in which, in the third, Paul's gospel is designed, by generating and sustaining the richly varied church, to announce to the principalities and powers that their time is up. This does not produce a fully realized eschatology, of course, and Ephesians 6 faces squarely the fact that there are battles still to be fought, battles which, though they may seem to be with flesh and blood, are in reality with the darker enemies that stand behind, enemies who will not be defeated until the time spoken of in 1 Corinthians 15. But the defensive armour which the Christian is given is itself borrowed from the victory of Jesus in his resurrection, so that spiritual warfare itself is seen as a kind of inaugurated eschatology, as the partial parallel with 1 Thessalonians 5 would strongly suggest.[18]

This brings us back to Romans. I noted in the previous chapter that Paul begins and ends the theological exposition of the letter with the strong note of Jesus as the Davidic Messiah, risen from the dead.[19] In fact, the whole introduction to the letter contains so many apparently counter-imperial signals that I find it impossible to doubt that both Paul and his first hearers and readers – in Rome, of all places! – would have picked up the message, loud and clear.[20] Jesus is the world's true Lord, constituted as such by his resurrection. He claims the whole world, summoning them to 'the obedience of faith', that obedient loyalty which outmatches the loyalty Caesar demanded. The summons consists of the 'gospel', a word which, as is now more widely recognized, contains the inescapable overtones *both* of the message announced by Isaiah's herald, the message of return from exile and the return of YHWH to Zion, *and* of the 'good news' heralded around the Roman world every time the anniversary of the emperor's accession, or his birthday, came round again. Paul comes to Rome, 'not ashamed of this gospel', as he says in 1.16, because – and here, clearly, every phrase counts – the gospel is God's *power* (that word again) to *salvation* (that word again) to all who *believe*, in other words, all those who are faithful and loyal; because in it, God's *dikaiosynē*, God's *iustitia*, God's saving covenant-based justice, is unveiled for all, the Jew first and also the Greek. Through the gospel, in other words, the one true God is claiming the allegiance of the entire world, since the gospel itself carries the same power which raised Jesus from the dead, unveiling the true salvation and the true justice before a world where those were already key imperial buzzwords.

This raises, of course, the question: is this a mere counter-imperial flourish, stuck on the front of a letter which is basically about something else? The answer must be no, though a full demonstration of this is impossible here. The question of the integration of this political dimension with all the other themes of Paul's theology, not least in Romans, is the really interesting meta-issue behind this whole investigation, and I can here only hint at the answer I think awaits us. But, for a start, let us try to see Romans in the following light. The result of the revelation of God's saving justice (chs. 1—4) is the creation of the worldwide family of faith promised to Abraham, the people whose sins have been forgiven and who have thereby been rescued from the world of paganism (ch. 1) in whose problems the Jews share equally (ch. 2). As a result, this new people enjoy peace (ch. 5) and freedom (ch. 6), within the larger metanarrative which Paul outlines at this point, the retelling of the Exodus. As in the Wisdom of Solomon, the retelling of the Exodus story in one form or another is a way of saying: this is how God rescues his people from pagan empires and all they stand for. Those who receive God's gift in the gospel will, Paul declares, share the sovereign reign of the Messiah over the world (5.17), a theme not sufficiently explored within Pauline theology. Paul, it seems, is himself integrating his theology of salvation from sin and death, here and hereafter, with his call to allegiance to Jesus, not Caesar, as lord. The retelling of the story of Israel in Romans 9—11, reaching its climax in Jesus the Messiah, serves from this point of view as a counter-story to the by now standard imperial narrative of Roman history reaching its climax in Augustus Caesar. And the ecclesiology of Romans 12—16 sustains the church as a community united across traditional boundaries, a community right under Caesar's nose in Rome, which is called to demonstrate in that unity the fact that the true God has acted and will act to create a new version of humanity before which Rome's attempts at uniting the world pale into insignificance. At virtually every point in the letter, all is focused once more on the cross of Jesus, the point at which Caesar did his worst and God did his uttermost.

What then about Romans 13.1–7? I have discussed the passage more fully in my commentary, and for our present purposes this discussion can be summarized in three points.

First, the passage belongs very closely with the end of chapter 12. Private vengeance is forbidden, but properly authorized officials have the duty to keep order and punish wrongdoers. This is a standard Jewish viewpoint, not far from a moderate Pharisaic line.

Second, Paul insists, over against normal imperial rhetoric, that earthly rulers are not themselves divine, but are answerable to the one true God. They are God's servants, and as servants they can expect to be held accountable. This passage actually represents a severe demotion of the rulers from the position they would have claimed to occupy.

Third, precisely because of all the counter-imperial hints Paul has given not only in this letter and elsewhere but indeed by his entire gospel, it is vital that he steer Christians away from the assumption that loyalty to Jesus would mean the kind of civil disobedience and revolution that merely reshuffles the political cards into a different order. The passage is closely integrated with the eschatological promise at the end of the chapter (13.11–14), which echoes the promise in the counter-imperial passage in 1 Thessalonians 5: the night is nearly over, the day is at hand. The main thing Paul wants to emphasize is that, even though Christians are the servants of the Messiah, the true lord, this does not give them carte blanche to ignore the temporary subordinates whose appointed task, whether (like Cyrus) they know it or not, is to bring at least a measure of God's order and justice to the world. The church must live as a sign of the kingdom yet to come, but since that kingdom is characterized by justice, peace and joy in the Spirit (14.17), it cannot be inaugurated in the present by violence and hatred.

There are, of course, plenty of other things to be said about this passage, but not here. I have said enough to locate Paul credibly both within the standard Jewish views of how to live within pagan empire and within the new world inaugurated by the gospel of the crucified and risen Messiah.

5. Conclusion

Even this all-too-brief survey has shown, I believe, that there are indeed echoes, and more than just echoes, of the rhetoric of imperial Rome in the writings of Paul. The material was available and widely known; Paul repeats his points sufficiently often for a credible volume to be attained both in individual passages and letters and in recurring themes; his critique coheres at all kinds of points with other themes in this theology; and the picture we thus get is, I suggest, enormously plausible historically. The history of interpretation remains, for interesting reasons, largely innocent of this way of reading him. But I think Paul himself would have been horrified if we ignored this dimension, and mightily relieved at the 'aha' which arises when, with these elements finally unveiled, we see his thought in the round. When I began to study Paul's theology of creation and covenant, Messiah and apocalyptic, I had no thought whatever of this political dimension. Likewise, most of the scholars who have recently drawn attention to the political dimension have eschewed any interest in Paul's wider theology. But I persist in thinking that these usually differentiated strands were in fact woven tightly together into the single fabric of his theology and life.

In order to see how that works out, we must take a step back, and look at that life, and that theology, through a set of different lenses. That is the task of the second part of this book.

Part II

STRUCTURES

5

Rethinking God

1. Introduction

In this and the next two chapters I offer an outline sketch of the shape of Paul's theology.

There has been enormous debate over the years about the proper way of arranging the various topics Paul talks about. All kinds of systems and arrangements have been tried. The familiar topics of reformation soteriology have often provided a framework, with the state of humankind, the nature of sin, death and the Law, the grace of God and the atoning death of Jesus as the major topics. This has produced the odd situation that other vital Pauline themes such as the resurrection, the place of Israel and even God himself have not been integrated into the overall structure. It is of course possible in theory that Paul had only incidental things to say on such topics, but even a nodding acquaintance with the letters suggests otherwise. Having often felt profoundly dissatisfied with the usual systems, I have wanted for some time to propose a fresh way of organizing Pauline theology, for which the earlier chapters in this book have been as it were preliminary studies.

The obvious place to begin is with the shape of classic Jewish theology. It is a measure of how little Paul's Jewish context was taken seriously in older formulations that this simply doesn't seem to have occurred to writers like, say, Rudolf Bultmann. Systematic theology has not been a Jewish concern in the same way that it has been a Christian concern, for reasons outside our present purpose. But when Jewish writers have taken it upon themselves to summarize what Jews believe, they have focused on two topics, with a third not far behind.[1] The main two are God and God's people: monotheism and election. When you put monotheism and election together, and then look at the present state of the world and of God's people, you will quickly come up with a third, namely eschatology. If there is one God, and if Israel is God's people, something is surely wrong: how is the one God going to fulfil his promises to his people, and indeed to the world? Hence the threefold pattern: one God, one people of God, one future for God's world. My proposal in this second main part of the book is that Paul's thought can best be understood, not as an abandonment of this framework, but as his redefinition of it around the Messiah and the Spirit. This chapter and the following two will explore these topics in turn, leaving the way clear for a final chapter which offers some concluding reflections and proposals.

Monotheism, election and eschatology are thus closely interrelated:

(1) The one God is revealed not only as the creator and sustainer of the world, but also precisely as the God of Israel, that is, the electing God, and also the God of that final judgment for which he, as creator and sustainer, must remain responsible.

(2) Election, as it becomes refocused on Jesus as Messiah, is seen as the personal self-revelation of the one God in action and, so to speak, in passion. As we have already seen, Paul's Christology binds the story of God and the story of Israel tightly together, and in doing so also gives eschatology its characteristically Christian shape: the long-awaited end has come forwards into the present, and has given the present time its peculiar character of now-and-not-yet.

(3) The coming end is itself guaranteed because of the justice of the one creator and covenant God. This eschatological vision is already revealed in Jesus the Messiah, and the energy by which the world and the church are moved from the present time to that ultimate future is the Spirit.

Each of the three topics is sliced through at right angles by three others, which we cannot develop in any detail in the present book but which form vital elements in the way Paul worked – that is, both the way his mind worked and the way he organized and conducted his whole life.

First, each of these redefinitions is rooted in a re-reading of Israel's scriptures.[2] This re-reading is not, however, a matter merely of typology, picking a few earlier themes and watching the same patterns repeating themselves, though this also happens often enough. As I have argued in the earlier chapters, Paul had in mind an essentially historical and sequential reading of scripture, in which the death and resurrection of the Messiah formed the unexpected but always intended climax of God's lengthy plan. Paul drew especially on the idea of a new exodus, and on a reading of Genesis, Deuteronomy, Isaiah and the Psalms in particular. In offering this fresh reading, he was regularly in at least implicit, and sometimes explicit, dialogue with alternative readings of the same scriptures, necessitating an essentially intra-Jewish, and sometimes intra-Christian, running controversy in favour of *this* fulfilment of scripture against other possible claims and agendas.

Second, in each case Paul's main polemical target is not Judaism, as has so often been thought, despite this running battle on the side, but paganism. He remained at this point a typical Jew, understanding paganism in terms of idolatry, immorality and the consequent corruption of God's good creation and of image-bearing humankind. At each point – God, God's people, God's future for the world – he offered a vision reshaped around Jesus and the Spirit, rooted in the Jewish scriptures, and claiming to be the reality of which paganism possessed a parody. We have already seen this to good advantage in Paul's Christian reworking of the Jewish critique of pagan empire; the same can be said, *mutatis mutandis*, of his critique of other aspects of paganism.

Third, each of these redefined doctrines came to expression in the task of preaching the gospel to the world and then of building up the church through prayer, personal visits and teaching, and letters themselves. Paul would have seen this not as an accidental or a secondary expression, but as the necessary context for their exploration. His detailed apostolic work was not merely incidental, the way he happened to devise or stumble upon for propagating a set of abstract truths. It was entailed by those very redefined truths themselves.

One final word of introduction. I suggest, though there is no space to follow this through, that Paul's redefined Jewish theology, resulting as it did in the redemption and renewal of human beings, gives him a robust epistemology in which, through worship, praise and prayer he is called to know and love the God who already knows and loves him, and through sharing the mind of the Messiah and the fresh insight of the Spirit he is called to know and love other human beings and the world. Thus the wisdom which Paul expounds in, for instance, Colossians 1 and 2 and 1 Corinthians 1—3 and 8.1–6 is itself the energy which drives the epistemology which sustains the theology. At this point, in fact, Paul's Christian epistemology merges imperceptibly into what today we call, however loosely, spirituality.

So to the theology itself. We begin with Paul's redefinition of the most central Jewish doctrine of all, that of the one God.

2. Monotheism: The Jewish Roots

There was, of course, more than one type of monotheism in the ancient world, as in the modern. People sometimes talk as if the word 'monotheism' always referred to the same kind of theology, but that is just as mistaken as the still common idea that the word 'God' itself is univocal. An obvious example of another kind of monotheism is pantheism, some form of which was well known in Paul's world through the various kinds of Stoicism: if everything is divine, or if divinity lives within everything, then there may be one divinity, but this is a very different kind of divinity to the one invoked by ancient Israel. Similarly, it is possible for those who go down the Epicurean road, with divinity (or divinities) and the world separated by a vast gulf, to land up with a kind of Deism where there is indeed only one God – but where this 'God' is very different from the passionately involved and compassionately committed God of Exodus, Isaiah or the Psalms. Within the twenty-first-century world of religious discourse, it is a matter of sensitive debate whether we should suppose that the one God revealed in Jesus is identical to the one God known in Judaism or the one God revealed in the Koran – or whether, to put that more carefully, the language used in these different traditions about the one God does in fact refer to the same being, even though the things predicated of God contain serious mutual incompatibilities (it is analytically true of the God of the Koran that he would not and could not have become incarnate in the form of a 'son', and that he neither would nor could have died on a cross). Whatever we say about that, my point is that Jewish monotheism of the sort that Paul knew when he was growing up is a particular type of monotheism, which elsewhere I and others have called *creational and covenantal monotheism*. The one God of Israel made the world and has remained in dynamic relationship with it; and this one God, in order to further his purposes within and for that world, has entered into covenant with Israel in particular.

This in turn allows for the characteristically Jewish view of the problem of evil. This is really a separate topic. But, just as any serious view of God and the world will include some integrated treatment of evil, so the ancient Jewish worldview in particular (in each of its bewildering varieties; let us not get stuck on the old *canard* of 'Judaism' versus 'Judaisms') includes a view of evil, flexible enough to be sustained through many variations, and belonging closely with monotheism, election and eschatology. Let me summarize crudely. Ancient Judaism, and the Christianity which came to birth from within it, can be contrasted with its two main contemporary rivals at the level of worldview: pantheism and Epicureanism.

Pantheism (of which Stoicism provided the main first-century variety) always has difficulty giving a sustained account of evil. If the world itself is divine, there ought to be no problem, and the answer to any problems that may be felt is to get more deeply in touch with the true nature of things, and of oneself. By contrast, Epicureanism (of which Deism is one modern expression) has no difficulty giving an account of evil, since the ontological gap between the divine and the world in which we live is so great that there is really nothing to be explained. Evil is simply part of where we are, a shabby, second-rate world, a long way away from the bliss of heaven. The only solution is then to enjoy the world where one can, and shrug one's shoulders where one cannot.

But within most varieties of Judaism, and certainly within those varieties upon which the early Christians drew, and which they re-thought around Jesus himself, neither of these was an option. There was one God, the creator, who had remained passionately and compassionately involved with the world, and had expressed that in the call of Israel; that, as we have seen, is the meaning of covenant and election. Evil is thus a far greater problem in Judaism than in either pantheism or Epicureanism, ancient or modern. That is why we have, within ancient Judaism, such works as Psalms 73 and 88 and, towering high above the rest with its summit in the clouds, the book of Job. Judaism, even under intense pressure, never quite gives up on the belief that evil – moral evil, societal evil, evil within the natural order itself – matters desperately to God, and that he will one day not only put the world to rights but somehow deal retrospectively with the horror, violence, degradation and decay which has so radically (from this point of view) infected creation, not least human beings, including Israel. The wolf will at the last lie down with the lamb, and the earth shall be full of the glory of God as the waters cover the sea. The question of *how* God is involved in the mess and shame of the world at the present time, and more particularly of how he will ultimately deal with it, often remains opaque, though we have suggested some of the larger themes in Chapters 2 and 3 above. Monotheism, election and eschatology are, at one level, all about the problem of evil.

Jewish analyses of evil regularly focus on idolatry, that is, the worship of someone or something other than the true God. Idolatry inevitably, in such analysis, leads to the failure of humans to reflect the image of the true God, that is, the failure to be genuinely human: this means 'missing-the-mark', *hamartia*, in other words, 'sin'. This analysis of evil regularly extends, within Law, prophets, writings and the continued thought of the second-Temple period, to a critique of the same flaws and failings within Israel itself. And it is this analysis of evil, in the pagan world and also, against the grain of election and covenant, within Israel itself, that sets the context for characteristically Jewish, characteristically monotheistic, solutions to the problem. Here the lines of thought converge, again and again, on the central themes of exile and restoration. Adam and Eve are expelled from the garden; Abraham is promised the Land. Jacob and his family are enslaved in Egypt; Moses and Joshua lead them through the Red Sea, the wilderness and the Jordan, home to their inheritance. David flees Jerusalem during Absalom's rebellion, and is brought back after a great but tragic victory. Israel is dragged away captive to Babylon, and then promised a return so glorious that the 'return from exile', when it happened, never quite matched the expectation. And it is *within* these great themes, not as a separate or detached theological reflection, that we find the sudden bright, yet still mysterious, flashes of a redemption which speaks of much more than the to-and-fro of ethnic migrations: of God ransoming his worshippers from Sheol, breathing his Spirit into lifeless skeletons, revealing his powerful Arm in the form of a Servant who is stricken for the people's transgressions. The problem of evil, as it appears within characteristically Jewish monotheism, and as it is given a second dimension within the covenant people themselves, receives –

or at least, is promised – a solution commensurate with the analysis. More of all this anon, especially in the next chapter.

Jewish monotheism, then, always ranged itself over against paganism, seeing the pagan world as embodying and expressing the failure of human beings to live as they were made to live, to reflect the image of their maker. When Israel looked back in folklore to the time of slavery in Egypt, it was envisaged in terms of living alongside an alien people clutching their gods – just as the ancient legends about Abraham saw him, before his call to leave home and follow God, as belonging to a thriving society of idol-worshippers. The promise of the land included the judgment on the wickedness of its present inhabitants and the repeated warnings to Israel not to copy them, warnings re-emphasized throughout the psalms, prophets and wisdom traditions. For many of the prophets, not least (in their different ways) Isaiah, Jeremiah and Daniel, this warning about and critique of paganism turns sharply against pagan empire in particular, with Babylon seen as the archetypal pagan system: idolatry raised to great height, embodied in great power, and working great evil not least against God's own people. Jewish monotheism in the Old Testament never remained a theoretical belief, an intellectual best guess. It was always at work, summoning Israel to worship the one true God and thus to be sharply distinguished from the nations all around – and, of course, turning the critical spotlight on Israel itself whenever it appeared to compromise with paganism, to live 'like all the nations'.

A fuller treatment would of course trace these strands of thought into Paul's own world in the first century. In particular, this monotheism is developed in the apocalyptic traditions, where it comes under considerable strain, with works like 4 Ezra putting God's credibility quite drastically on the line. In the wisdom traditions which emerge in the Wisdom of Solomon, the nations are warned, as in Daniel, that true wisdom, including the wisdom that rulers need in order to govern, comes from the one true God – and that this God will judge those who forget this and, going their own way, oppress his people. One should really also, at this point, explore traditions like the Eighteen Benedictions, in which Jewish monotheism comes to its most characteristic expression in praise, worship and commitment. There are vast tracts of rabbinic exposition of

Israel's monotheism which ought to be considered, and would take a chapter, if not a book, in themselves. It is also important to explore the ways in which monotheism received other characteristic expressions, not least the long tradition of resistance to pagan rule which spoke, in good monotheistic language, of God and only God becoming king, an idea which had been redefined by and around Jesus but emphatically not abandoned.[3] But, though it is of course vital to ground Paul not simply in the scriptures but in the traditions of his own day, it is noticeable that when we analyse the scriptural texts to which he most frequently refers we find that they regularly come from the most solidly and explicitly monotheistic passages – Genesis, Deuteronomy, the Psalms, Isaiah, and so on. This is no accident. He understands himself as a monotheist of this sort, within this tradition, and we must understand this claim if we are to grasp what he thought he was doing.

Jewish monotheism had already, by Paul's time, developed ways of speaking of the action of the one God within Israel and the world. God spoke and things happened, showing his creative Word at work. God breathed his Spirit into human nostrils, and had promised to pour out his Spirit in fresh ways on Israel and the world. God had promised to dwell in the Temple through the Shekinah, his glorious tabernacling presence. God had acted in creation by his Wisdom, and this Wisdom had continued to guide Israel in particular, though also all who sought it. Supremely, of course, God had revealed his way, his will and his wisdom itself to Israel through the Torah. It is hard to say how far any of these expressions of the activity and purpose of the one true God had developed by Paul's day into an ontological statement; actually, it is hard to determine what would count, or how we would know. But it seems clear to me that they were not seen as challenges to what Judaism meant by monotheism itself. Once again, it is a sign of Paul's intention to be and remain a firm Jewish-style monotheist that he draws on these specific traditions and develops his view of Jesus and the Spirit in dialogue, sometimes polemical dialogue, with them. *Telos gar nomou Christos*: the Messiah is both the goal and the end of Torah.[4] But this has brought us to the point where we must look at his redefinition.

3. Monotheism and Christology

There are many places where Paul demonstrates a clear and obvious adherence to Jewish-style monotheism, without any particularly striking redefinition. He refers to the oneness of God as a natural baseline in two crucial arguments, Romans 3 and Galatians 3. He praises the one God, the creator whom much of the world has spurned (Romans 1). He expounds the resurrection as the ultimate act of new creation by the God who made it in the first place (Romans 4; Romans 8; 1 Corinthians 15). He declares, without a shadow of pagan or pantheistic divinizing of creation, that food is good, marriage and sex are good, the created order is good, and that humans ought to enjoy them as what they are – that is, as parts of God's good creation – without worshipping them. When faced (in other words) with the chance to move towards an ontological dualism, he robustly refuses. That is the route to a cheap and shallow ethic (the world is a bad place, so stay away from it; human bodies are evil, so never gratify them), and whatever we say about Paul's exhortations to Christian behaviour they are never cheap or shallow. This could be shown in considerably more detail, but my main purpose here is to speak about the way in which, within this framework which he could take for granted and draw on at will, he accomplished his radical redefinitions.

We begin with those redefinitions of monotheism which turn out to have Jesus in the middle of them.[5] This deeply paradoxical theme – paradoxical, at least, from the point of view of Jewish critics ancient and modern, and of post-Enlightenment biblical scholarship in general – can be seen to great advantage in several passages about which much more could be and has been said. I begin with one whose complexity has sometimes put readers off the scent but which expresses in a few verses a good deal of what Paul wishes to say about Jesus, and which locates him, and these ideas, emphatically within Jewish-style monotheism. I refer to Romans 10.5–13.[6]

I shall have more to say in the next chapter about Paul's treatment of Deuteronomy 30 in Romans 10.5–8. Suffice it to say here that Paul is reading Deuteronomy, as other writers in his period had done (Baruch on the one hand, 4QMMT on the other), as laying out a historical programme which Israel was going to follow. If they obeyed Torah, then blessings would result; if they disobeyed, curses would be meted out, the ultimate curse being exile itself. But then, if they turned back to YHWH with a whole heart and mind, he would restore their fortunes and bring them back from exile – an event which, for Baruch, MMT and many other second-Temple writers, has clearly not yet happened. That will be the time of covenant renewal and redemption. In particular, it will be characterized by God bringing Torah near to Israel so that, instead of seeming high up in heaven or way beyond the sea in its unfulfillability, it will be written on their hearts.

What has this got to do with Christology and monotheism? Everything, it seems. Paul reads this passage, a prediction of the ultimate return from exile, as a passage about what God has now done, not through Torah, but through the Messiah. The new Exodus, the great covenant renewal, has happened in and through him. Instead of Torah, it is he, acclaimed and believed in Christian faith, who is now the badge of God's renewed people. 'If you confess with your lips that Jesus is Lord, and believe in your heart that God raised him from the dead, you will be saved' (10.9). Among the many points which Paul develops in the next four verses, we notice particularly the way he uses the word *kyrios*, Lord. 'The same Lord is Lord of all,' he writes, 'rich in mercy to all who call upon him, for' – and then he quotes the new covenant passage from Joel – '"all who call on the name of the Lord will be saved".'[7] It is frequently noticed, but must be highlighted again here, that Paul takes the *kyrios* of the Septuagint, in passages where he is very well aware that in context it referred to YHWH himself, and understands it as a reference to Jesus. We should not miss, either, the strong point, that verse 13 is thus answering the question of verse 1: how are Paul's fellow Jews to be saved? Why, by believing in the *kyrios* through whom the one God has fulfilled his promises in Deuteronomy 30. In him, after all, has been revealed God's covenant plan, the *dikaiosynē theou*, to which we shall return.

The strong and high Christology of Romans 10.5–13 is in fact already foreshadowed in 9.5.[8] This is of course controversial, but as I and others have argued it makes excellent sense not only in itself but in the light of Romans 9—11 as a whole to read the passage as an affirmation that Jesus is not only Israel's Messiah according to the flesh but also 'God over all, blessed for ever, Amen'. The main arguments against this reading are not so much exegetical as a priori theological: Paul 'could not have said such a thing' in the light of what he says elsewhere. I hope that the rest of my argument in the present section will serve to undermine that objection. And if I am right here we have an instance not only of Paul referring to Jesus as 'God' but of his doing so in a very Jewish way, invoking a blessing on him, as he does more straightforwardly in relation to the creator God in another strongly monotheistic passage early on in the letter (1.20).

Perhaps the most famous passage where Paul refers to Jesus as *kyrios*, in a context where he was certainly thinking of a Septuagint passage, is Philippians 2.6–11.[9] It is now, I think, largely recognized that this passage does indeed express a very early, very Jewish and very high Christology, in which Paul understands the human being Jesus to be identical with one who from all eternity was equal with the creator God, and who gave fresh expression to what that equality meant by incarnation, humiliating suffering, and death. The 'therefore' of verse 9 is crucial: Jesus is now exalted to the position of supreme honour, sharing the glory that the one God will not share with another, *because* he has done what only the one God can do. The logic of the poem forces us to acknowledge that Paul knows perfectly well, in quoting Isaiah 45.23 in the closing verses, just how enormous a claim he is making. In that passage, one of the most fiercely monotheistic statements in the Old Testament, YHWH declares that he is God, and there is no other; to YHWH and him alone every knee will bow and every tongue swear. (Paul quotes the same passage in Romans 14.10, in the context of the universal sovereignty and coming judgment of God through Jesus.) What he has done in Philippians, in addition to a great many other things (not least, as we saw in the previous chapter, upstaging Caesar), is to write a poem whose roots are deep in Jewish monotheism, and to place Jesus in the middle of it. Or, to put it the other way round, he has written a poem in praise of the humiliation and exaltation of Jesus, both for its own sake and as a model of the mutual submission required in the church, and he has expressed that praise in terms characteristic of ancient Israel's praise of the one true God.

The same is true in another well-known passage, 1 Corinthians 8.6.[10] Here again the context is all-important. Paul is facing the question of how to live as a Christian within pagan society, more specifically, whether one may or may not eat meat that has been offered to idols. His opening comments on the matter, after an initial remark about knowledge and love, show where he is coming from: we Christians, he says, are Jewish-style monotheists, not pagan polytheists. We know that no idol has any real ontological existence, and that there is 'no God but one'.[11] You could scarcely get clearer than that. Paul is well aware – he could hardly not be, after the places where he had lived and worked – that there were many so-called gods, and many so-called lords, out there on the streets. But the regular beliefs of pagan polytheism were, for him, decisively challenged by the Jewish claim about the one true God. Who was this one God, and how did Israel most characteristically acknowledge him? He was the God who revealed himself to Israel's ancestors not least at the time of the Exodus, and he was worshipped and acknowledged supremely in the daily prayer, the Shema: Hear, O Israel, YHWH our God, YHWH is one – or, in the Septuagint, *kyrios ho theos hēmōn, kyrios heis estin.*[12] Within his monotheistic argument, to make a monotheistic point, Paul quotes this, the best-known of all Jewish monotheistic formulae, and once again he puts Jesus into the middle of it. For us, he says, there is one God, one Lord. More specifically, 'for us there is one God, the father, from whom are all things and we to him, and one Lord, Jesus the Messiah, through whom are all things and we through him'. He has quoted the Septuagint formula, glossing *theos*, that is, *elohim*, with a phrase about the Father as the supreme creator and goal of all, and glossing *kyrios*, that is, YHWH, with a phrase about Jesus the Messiah as God's agent in both creation and redemption. Looking outside the immediate impact of this, we observe that he has thereby done with Jesus what was sometimes done with the figure (personified or personal?) of Wisdom, the one through whom the creator made the world, the true content of God's self-revelation in Torah.

What follows from this explosive redefinition of the Shema in 1 Corinthians 8.6 is equally remarkable in its own way. Once Jesus is established at the heart of the vision of the one true God, serving and following this God will involve living according to the pattern of *love*. That is why Paul's opening remark in the chapter sets up a contrast between mere 'knowledge', *gnōsis*, and love itself. This, too, is why he now goes on, in the rest of the chapter, to insist that self-sacrificial love for one's neighbour is the primary consideration when working out how to live within a pagan environment.

From 1 Corinthians 8 it is a short and natural step to Colossians 1.15–20. We have already looked at this passage in Chapter 2. Suffice it to say here that this spectacular poem is a classic expression of Jewish-style monotheism, of creation and redemption as the work of one and the same God, and that throughout the poem, modelled carefully and beautifully on a complex understanding of Proverbs 8 and Genesis 1, we find Jesus taking the role of God's agent in all that he does, the role once more of Wisdom.

All this and more is summed up for Paul in one of the titles for Jesus which, though he does not use it very often, comes with great force when he does. The phrase 'son of God' was known in Judaism as a reference to angels, but it is the two other uses which indicate where Paul sees its roots: Israel itself as 'son of God' (not least in Exodus 4.22), and the Messiah as 'son of God' in 2 Samuel 7.14 and Psalms 2.7 and 89.27. What Paul has done is to take this idea and fill it with new content, without losing the messianic meaning and the cognate one of representing Israel. What has happened in, to and through Jesus has convinced Paul that hidden within the divinely intended meaning of Messiahship was God's determination not just *to send someone else* to do what had to be done but to come himself to do it in person. Only so can we make sense of passages like Romans 5.6–11, where the death of Jesus (precisely as the son of God, as in 8.3 and 8.32) expresses more clearly than anything else the *love* of God. This can only be so if Jesus is understood as the very embodiment of the one God.

If we enquire how Paul came to use this phrase for Jesus with this meaning, I believe there are two answers which work together. On the one hand, Jesus himself had used similar 'son of God' language of himself, and in the memory of the earliest church that cannot have been irrelevant in determining early Christian usage.[13] On the other hand, just as Paul, struggling to find ways of thinking the unthinkable and saying the unsayable, seems to have settled on the word 'father' for God the creator, even when as in 1 Corinthians 8.6 he is not going to use the word 'son' of Jesus, but rather (because of the text he is quoting) the word 'lord', so it became natural for him to speak of Jesus as 'God's son' with the meaning, not just of God's messianic agent for Israel and the world, but of God's second self, God's ultimate self-expression as a human being.

This is seen to good advantage in two chapters we shall explore presently in looking at the way in which the Spirit, too, forms part of Paul's redefinition of Jewish monotheism. But in summing up this section on the christological redefinition of monotheism we must inevitably say a word about the cross. For Paul this was of course the ultimately shocking and ultimately glorious thing: that in becoming human to fulfil his own promises, Israel's God, the creator, had chosen to die on a cross. The cross became, for Paul, the fullest possible revelation of both the love and the justice of God, and then, in its outworking, the extraordinary saving power of God, defeating the powers that held people captive in pagan darkness and breaking the long entail of human sin. The cross is the climactic moment in Paul's redefinition of election, and there will be more to say about it under that heading in the next chapter. It is, for Paul, the ultimate point where the ancient problem of evil, as seen in characteristically Jewish ways, is addressed head on by the one God. The crucifixion and death of Jesus (we should not get stuck here on the presence or absence of the word *stauros*, cross, in this or that argument) is not merely added on to Paul's Christology but the point where it is all going, or, from another viewpoint, the point where it all began. This is why, in the climactic passage Romans 3.21–26, it is the crucifixion of the Messiah that reveals the *dikaiosynē theou*, the faithfulness of the covenant God to his promise, the faithfulness of the creator to his creation, the justice which, like mountains, soars high above the multiple injustices of the world. The cross is the place where Paul sees God's justice fully displayed; his Christology, seen as the revision of Jewish-style monotheism, is the context within which we can best understand it. This leads the eye naturally to one of Paul's remarkable periphrastic statements about God: we believe, he says, in 'the God who raised Jesus our Lord from the dead, who was handed over for our trespasses and raised for our justification'.[14] This, coming at the close of a passage where Paul has been emphasizing the way in which Abraham acknowledged the true God and worshipped him and recognized his power, by contrast with the pagan world which did none of those things, has enormous force as a further summary redefinition of the true God by means of a reference to Jesus. As every serious reader of Paul has long recognized, though not so many have explored to the full, the cross of Jesus the Messiah stands at the heart of Paul's vision of the one true God.

4. Monotheism and the Spirit

The second branch of Paul's redefinition is closely allied with the first. Central to this theme are two passages of great power and concentrated theological energy, in which a classically Jewish monotheism is expressed in relation to Jesus and the Spirit together.[15]

The first is Galatians 4.1–7. Paul has developed in the previous chapter the picture of God keeping Israel as a young child under the somewhat fierce tutelage of the household slave, the official babysitter, namely the Torah. This tutelage was designed, he says, until the time of maturity, the time when Jews and Gentiles alike would be brought into the one family, the single family promised to Abraham. Then, at the start of chapter 4, he takes this picture and holds it up to the light. The young son, even though he is heir to the whole estate, is kept under tutors and guardians until he grows up. So we, he says daringly, were kept in a form of slavery under the elements of the world. But what does Jewish tradition say about Israel, the heir to God's promises, being kept in slavery under pagan rule? Israel tells, of course, the story of the Exodus, and so does Paul, precisely at this point. When the right time arrived, the time of fulfilment, God set his people free. He did this, more specifically, by first sending his own son, born of a woman, born under the Law, to redeem those under the Law, and to make them his true children ('Israel is my son, my firstborn; so let my people go'). Here we see that interplay of themes between the messianic son and God's redeemed people as his 'sons' of which I wrote earlier (and which is of course obscured in a non-gender-specific translation), and with the precise new meaning that the messianic 'son' is the one who expresses and embodies God's saving intention. This leads to the decisive verse 7: 'because you are sons, God has sent the Spirit of his son into our hearts crying "Abba, Father". So you are no longer slaves but sons, and if sons, then heirs through the Messiah.'

Paul's main aim here is, obviously, to reinforce his central point, that the Galatian Christians are already complete in Christ, and do not need to take upon themselves the yoke of Torah. But as he does this we can watch him also developing the Jewish monotheistic picture of God in a spectacular new way. This is the full, fresh revelation of the God of Abraham, the God of the Exodus: he is now to be known, worshipped, and trusted as the God who sends the son and the God who sends the Spirit of the son. Paul knows exactly what he has done, because in the very next passage, by way of ramming home his basic appeal, he speaks of the Galatians having now come 'to know God, *or rather to be known by him*'. This son-sending and Spirit-sending God is the one true God, and they have entered into a relationship of mutual knowing with him, with God taking and retaining the initiative. How, then, can they want to go back to the 'weak and beggarly elements', the *stoicheia*, the local or tribal deities who had previously kept them under lock and key? We note in passing that Paul is here lining up the Torah along with the pagan landlord-gods; the contrast is between the true God, now fully revealed in the new Exodus as YHWH had been freshly revealed in the first Exodus, and the pagan gods. This is a typically Jewish thing to do, to line up the Exodus-God against the pagan deities; and Paul has described the Exodus-God as the son-sending, Spirit-sending God. It is as though he is saying, you either have this God, known in this way, or you have paganism. From here on – and I believe Galatians is one of the earliest Christian documents we possess – one might conclude that if the doctrine of the Trinity had not come into existence it would be necessary to invent it.

This remarkable passage leads the eye naturally to Romans 8, where again Paul draws heavily on the motif and the language of the Exodus.[16] God's people, set free from slavery, must not think of going back to it, but must rely on the presence and leading of God as they go on to their inheritance. Within the original Exodus-story, of course, the people were given the tabernacling presence of God, despite their rebellion and sin, as their guide and companion. In Paul's retelling of the story, the Spirit takes the place of the Shekinah, leading the people to the promised land, which turns out to be, not 'heaven' as in much Christian mistelling of the story ('heaven' is not mentioned here or in any similar passages), but the new, or rather the renewed, creation, the cosmos which is to be liberated from its own slavery, to experience its own 'exodus'. The Spirit then forms (8.24) the first-fruits, the sign of a larger harvest to come; this is cognate with the idea of the 'guarantee', the *arrabōn*, the initial down payment which ensures that the rest will be paid at its proper time.[17] The redemption of human beings, here as in some other parts of the New Testament, is not merely for their own sake, but so that, through them and their new life, the one God can bring his wise order and redemption to the rest of the world. This, too, is part of typical Jewish monotheism.

The development of this theme, like all the rest of Romans 8, grows out of the opening paragraph, verses 1–11, and out of verses 3 and 4 in particular. Here, very close to Galatians 4, we find the son and the Spirit together being God's agents in fulfilling his promises. Now, however, this work is explicitly lined up over against that of Torah, whose failure to give the life it promised has been set out so spectacularly in chapter 7. 'What the Torah could not do . . . God has done, sending his own son in the likeness of sinful flesh and as a sin-offering, in order that the just requirement of Torah might be fulfilled in us who walk not according to the flesh but according to the Spirit' (8.3–4). Without offering a full exegesis of this dense and remarkable double verse, we simply note that Paul is again working from within the framework of Jewish-style monotheism, seeing the Spirit alongside the son as the agents of the one God, doing what Wisdom was to do, doing what Torah wanted to do but could not.[18] Here we are close to that simultaneous affirmation of Torah and bypassing of Torah which has for so long kept Pauline scholars awake at nights.

Once we start to see this pattern, of the son and the Spirit together redefining Jewish monotheism, we notice similar things all over the place. In Romans 10.13, with which I began the treatment of Christology, Paul draws on a passage from Joel which elsewhere in the New Testament is used in relation to the outpouring of the Spirit. The fact that this becomes explicit in two closely cognate passages – Romans 2.25–29 and 2 Corinthians 3 – ought to alert us to the presence of the Spirit under the compressed argument of Romans 10 itself. In 1 Corinthians 12.4–6, Paul declares, over against the chaos of pagan-style worship, that when the Spirit of the living God is at work there must be genuine unity. But even here, where he is wanting to stress this unity against the wrong sort of diversity, he says it in three separate ways: there are varieties of gifts, but the same Spirit; varieties of service, but the same Lord; varieties of working, but it is the same God who accomplishes all in all (that last phrase a favourite monotheistic slogan, which reappears in an eschatological setting in 1 Corinthians 15.28 and Ephesians 1.23). The unity in diversity which the church must exhibit in its worship is grounded in and modelled on that unity in diversity which Paul simply names, without further argument or discussion, as Spirit, Lord and God.

We see this same theology worked out in practice in Paul's various references to the way in which the gospel, the royal proclamation of Jesus as Messiah and Lord, actually works or functions. I have often reflected on the strangeness of the task to which Paul devoted his life: telling pagans that there was a single creator God rather than a multiplicity of gods was bad enough, but adding that this God had made himself known in a crucified Jew, who had then been raised from the dead, was bound to cause hoots of derision, and, if Acts is to be believed, sometimes did. Yet Paul found that when he told this story, when he proclaimed that this Jesus was indeed the world's true Lord, people (to their great surprise, no doubt) found this announcement making itself at home in their minds and hearts, generating the belief that it was true, and transforming their lives with a strange new presence and power.

Paul has various ways of talking about all this, and most of them employ the language of the Spirit. No one can say 'Jesus is Lord', he says, unless by the Spirit (1 Corinthians 12.3, the passage immediately before the threefold statement just mentioned). He has other ways of saying this: the gospel (i.e. the announcement of Jesus as Lord) is God's power to salvation for those who believe (Romans 1.16); the fact that the Spirit is not mentioned explicitly in that passage should not lead us to imagine that we are in a different seam of thought. Closely related statements are found in the first letter to Thessalonica. First, he declares in 1.5 that the gospel did not come in word only but in power, and in the Holy Spirit, and in full conviction. This does not imply that the 'word' is not itself powerful, because he can speak in the next verse of the word, somewhat as in Isaiah 40.8 or 55.11, as a personified force doing its own work. This goes with the strong language about 'the word of the cross' in 1 Corinthians 1.18 and elsewhere. Then in 1 Thessalonians 2.13 he makes the point more explicit: 'When you received the word which you heard from us,' he says, 'you did not receive it as merely the word of human beings but, as it truly is, the word of God which is at work in you who believe.' In referring thus to the 'word' doing its own work, he is speaking as a typical Jewish monotheist; and, when he desires to explain this regular point more fully, he draws as we have seen on the language of the Spirit. Paul believed that the Spirit was at work when the word of the gospel was announced, and that this event was the characteristic way in which the one true God was claiming both Gentiles and Jews as part of the family of the Messiah, Jesus.

As is well known, Paul uses a variety of language about the Spirit. Sometimes he refers to the Spirit of God; sometimes the Spirit of the Messiah; sometimes the Spirit of Jesus. In one or two quite confusing passages, such as Romans 8.9–11, he switches almost kaleidoscopically between Messiah and Spirit, and various expressions for both. But in both major passages and almost casual asides we can see that, broadly speaking, Paul has done with the Spirit what he did with the Messiah. He has seen them both as poles around which to redefine the traditional Jewish doctrine of the one God.

To conclude these two sections, and to point on to the next one, we simply note one of the most splendidly Jewish passages of praise and prayer in the New Testament, that in Ephesians 1.3–14. It is in form a typical *berakah*, a prayer of blessing to the one God for his mighty acts in creation and redemption. In a letter which consciously celebrates the gospel victory over the principalities and powers of the pagan world, it invokes the God of Israel and claims his power over the whole world. And the way in which this is done is, at every stage, 'in the Messiah' – a phrase repeated, with variations, five times, with numerous other occurrences of 'in him' or 'in whom'. As in Philippians 2, what God does in and through the Messiah results in the praise of his own glory; and what God has done, according to this prayer, is to accomplish the new Exodus, the great 'redemption', in fulfilment of the plan stretching back to creation itself and on to the renewal of all things. Once again Paul (if it is he; if not, someone thinking remarkably like him) speaks of the word of truth, the gospel of their salvation, and of being sealed with the Spirit as the guarantee. Here are the great themes of Jewish monotheism, celebrated in a prayer whose every clause has been rethought around Jesus the Messiah, and whose life-giving message focuses on the gift of the Spirit. I do not say that all this counts as an argument for Pauline authorship. But if someone else wrote this passage, and if Paul had been asked whether it was a fair summary of what he had been saying in so many other passages, he would certainly have agreed that it was.

5. Scriptural Roots, Pagan Targets, Practical Work

A full account of Paul's redefined monotheism would need, as I said at the start of this chapter, to explore three things in detail: (a) his fresh engagement with Israel's scriptures, showing the elements of continuity and discontinuity with other readings of the same material at roughly the same time; (b) his articulation of the point in explicit opposition to the paganism(s) of the day; and (c) the way in which this redefinition played out in the actual life-setting of his day-to-day work of evangelism and looking after the young churches. Space forbids more than a cursory glance at each of these, an agenda for further work.

Paul himself offers various summaries of how his message relates to Israel's scriptures: the fresh revelation of God's covenant faithfulness is 'apart from Torah, though Torah and prophets bear witness to it' (Romans 3.21); 'the things that were written long ago were written for our instruction, so that through patience and through the encouragement of the scriptures we might have hope' (Romans 15.4). Paul draws frequently on the Exodus narrative, now to be recapitulated in the new Exodus, the real return from exile promised in Deuteronomy 30 and still awaited by many in his own day. He seems to have held in his mind a grand narrative about God, Israel and the world, and when faced with the events concerning Jesus he came to believe that this narrative had reached its appointed climax. How this played out in other areas we shall examine in the subsequent chapters; but central to my proposal here is that Paul believed that, just as Israel's God had been revealed in a new way when fulfilling his promises in the Exodus, so now this same God had been revealed in a new way, a full and final way, in fulfilling his new-Exodus promises by his son and his Spirit. The place where this narrative is laid out most obviously, in implicit dialogue with all kinds of other second-Temple Jewish retellings, is Romans 9 and 10, where Paul traces the story of God and his purposes through the patriarchs and the Exodus to the warnings of the prophets and the eventual failure of Israel, leading (in good Deuteronomic fashion) to the point where God at last restores the fortunes of his people – with the striking, dramatic new twist that God has now done this through the Messiah and the Spirit.

This retelling of the story of Israel, and Israel's God in particular, was bound to lead Paul into conflict, by reflex as it were, with other Jewish retellings of his day. His emphasis on the oneness of God in Romans 3 and Galatians 3 was in both cases a way of emphasizing that this God desired a single family, the one now created in Christ; we shall return to this in the next chapter. There, too, we shall deal at more length with the best known of his polemical targets, namely the Law. We have seen at various points that what he says about Christ and the Spirit as the key elements of the self-expression of the one God was bound to upstage Torah even at that level, over against all attempts in Judaism to make Torah almost an ontological extension of the being of the one God. The frequent attempts to summarize this move by saying that either Christ or the Spirit, or both, have replaced Torah in Paul's theology do not get to the heart of it. Paul has a clear and positive view of Torah. Even when it is performing a negative task, it remains God's Law, holy and just and good (Romans 7). What it cannot do – and, in the mysterious purposes of God, what it was never actually intended to do – was to give the life it had promised. To elevate it ontologically into a self-expressive part of the one true God himself, as some Jews of Paul's day were beginning to do (and as Ben-Sira 24 had done two centuries earlier), is to give it a role to which it does indeed point but which is reserved for the son and for the Spirit of the son.

This brings us to the true polemical targets of Paul's redefined monotheism, which as one might expect with such a very Jewish doctrine were the divinities, systems and behaviour patterns of paganism (as seen both in the pagan world and, as highlighted already by the prophets, within Israel itself). We do not possess many hints, certainly not in the letters, of what exactly Paul used to say when doing primary evangelism, but we can detect in various places the kind of thing we must assume him to have said. The creator God was the true God, now made known in Jesus the Messiah, his son, who would come as judge of all things; in this light, pagan deities, their shrines, temples, statues and hierarchies, were a bunch of shams, unreal gods who could still enslave people but had no power to save them.

This is said most clearly in 1 Thessalonians 1.9–10. 'You turned to God from idols, to serve a living and true God, and to wait for his son from heaven, whom he raised from the dead, Jesus who delivers us from the coming wrath.' The resurrection of the son of God had given new focus and energy to the monotheistic proclamation which Saul of Tarsus might have made, prior to his conversion, to any pagan prepared to give him a hearing. This is the belief, obviously, which lies behind his discussion of pagan temples in 1 Corinthians 8 and 10.

More specifically, Paul's redefined monotheism gave him a powerful stance over against the various 'powers of the world'. There is no time here for the full consideration that this topic deserves, but we may note that there is plenty of room, within the Jewish-style monotheism redefined around Christ and Spirit, for a serious analysis on his part both of the existence of principalities and powers in the world – in other words, this does not itself compromise monotheism, as has sometimes been thought – and also for the view that they have been defeated in the death and resurrection of the Messiah, with this defeat then being implemented by the Spirit in new creation in the future and in Christian living (anticipating that new creation) in the present. The western thought of our own period has often become confused at this point, because Paul's thought moves to and fro, in ways natural to him but strange to us, between what we think of as purely spiritual powers, right up to sin and death themselves, and the obviously earthly rulers who crucified Jesus (1 Corinthians 2.8). Somewhere in the middle, touching both, we should locate the shadowy *stoicheia*, of whom we have already briefly spoken.[19] What binds them all together is that they all alike rule over human beings, and over the rest of God's world for that matter, through the power and threat of corruption, decay and death itself. As the Wisdom of Solomon saw so clearly, earthly tyrants rule by establishing a kind of concordat with death. Caesar rules through the power of sin and death, and they rule through him. The point of Paul's redefined monotheism, by contrast, is that the resurrection of Jesus is the beginning of that new creation in which God's power over death itself is the means whereby creation is reaffirmed as good.

We thus arrive at Paul's nuanced critique of paganism. Just as his reaffirmation of Jewish monotheism did not mean that he did not have a sharp critique of how it worked out in practice, so his head-on confrontation with paganism did not mean that he was not able to affirm and reuse elements of it within his own thought.

As he says, he 'takes every thought captive to obey the Messiah' (2 Corinthians 10.5), and when it comes even to pagan political rulers he is clear that God wants the world to be ruled in an orderly way (Romans 13.1–7; Colossians 1.15–20), since the alternative is chaos come again. Confrontation does not mean dualism.

We see this worked out in a famous passage not in the letters but in Acts, namely the Areopagus Address of Acts 17.22–31. I take it, as I said in a previous chapter, that this represents an extremely compressed version of what Paul might have said on such an occasion. Much Pauline scholarship in the last generations has ignored this speech, for the fairly good reason that it comes from the author of Acts and not from Paul himself directly, and for the very bad reason that it says a lot of things which the scholarship in question was not prepared to allow Paul to be interested in. But when we begin at the beginning in the study of his theology, that is, with the Jewish doctrine of monotheism and its Christian redefinition, the speech makes a great deal of sense as a summary of exactly the kind of thing Paul might well have said. Here we see (a theme that could well be explored at more length) that his redefinition has enabled him to attain a stability in his theology: as well as affirming and exploiting the idea of an Altar to an Unknown God, and quoting approvingly from the pagan poet Aratus ('for we are also his offspring'), Paul can cheerfully sweep away the whole tradition of temples and images for which Athens was the wonder of the world ('the Almighty does not live in houses made with hands'); he can affirm what has to be affirmed in both the Stoic and the Epicurean traditions (God is very close to us, yet also quite different from us), while insisting on the very Jewish view that the true God is both the creator and the sustainer of the cosmos and longs to enter into relationship with his human creatures. And, with an irony not always noted, he can robustly call the highest court in the land to a higher justice yet, the justice of the true God who will bring just judgment to the world through the man he has appointed, Jesus, whom he raised from the dead. This whole sequence of thought has so many points of contact with so much of Paul's own writing – to look no further, the last point fits snugly alongside Romans 1.3–4 and 2.16 – that we should not doubt its substantial fidelity to his thought. It would be possible from this point, though not here, to move out into the wider pagan world of Paul's day and show how at point after point he effectively takes on and upstages the claims and systems of paganism in the name, and for the glory, of the one God of Israel, the God now revealed through Jesus and the Spirit.

Alongside Paul's fresh reading of the Jewish scriptures, and his continued though nuanced confrontation with paganism, we should note, for completeness, the way in which his redefined monotheism worked itself out in his actual life and work. Wayne Meeks, in a famous study of the sociology of Paul's communities, noted the way in which the little churches were an expression of monotheism itself: it is pleasantly paradoxical that a work of robust sociology should have been one of the first places where this central theological topic was reintroduced to the world of contemporary Pauline studies.[20] The point is that when people come to believe in one true God over against the divinities worshipped within their surrounding culture, they will naturally form different kinds of groupings, and as Paul went about preaching this one God he must have known, from experience if not a priori, that the result was bound to be the creation of cells, and networks, which would be regarded as suspicious or even downright subversive within the world of his day. His redefined monotheism shaped his own life of prayer (note his many invocations of God in terms of God-and-Jesus), his own passionate commitment to sanctity (the Jewish call to holiness undergirded by the achievement of Jesus and energized by the Spirit), and his cheerful and energetic public preaching: if there really was one God, and Jesus was his son, and the Spirit of this God, this Jesus, was at work through the word of the gospel, then the proclamation of this God and his 'good news' could never be a matter of offering a secret or private recipe either for a new kind of spirituality or a new method for obtaining post-mortem bliss. Content determined form; belief shaped the mode of address. And once the proclamation had been made, and the word had begun its strange work in human hearts and lives, that same redefined monotheism generated communities of a particular shape, demanding a particular kind of pastoral supervision. Much of Paul's letters, and the glimpses of actual face-to-face ministry we get through them, can profitably be analysed under this heading.

6. Conclusion

There is, clearly, much here to be explored further. I hope I have at least said enough in this chapter both to start the ball rolling as we contemplate the Jewish theology of Paul's day and the ways in which he redefined it, and to suggest ways in which well-known themes can be brought into fresh coherence when organized in this manner. In the next chapter we move to the doctrine of God's people, the doctrine of election, which will inevitably raise the question of what Paul meant by justification. I hope that by setting out the groundwork like this we will be able to see more clearly that this vital doctrine, too, is concerned not only with human beings and their fate but with the way in which the God of Israel is creating a people from, and for, the whole world.

6

Reworking God's People

1. Introduction

Paul's rethinking of the meaning of the word 'God' dovetails naturally with his rethinking of what it meant to be God's people. And, just as the belief in the one God was not simply a matter of working out intellectual puzzles but also (necessarily, granted who this one God was) a matter of worship, praise, prayer and loyal service, so the belief in God's people was not simply a matter of theory but also (necessarily, granted who this people was) a matter of apostolic work to found and nurture communities of faith. That is why, whereas I had provisionally entitled this chapter 'Rethinking God's People', I have now settled on 'reworking'. For Paul, the redefinition involved was not just something he theorized about, but something he did.

We follow the same plan as the previous chapter. I begin with a brief sketch of what election meant within first-century Judaism. The bulk of the chapter will then be taken up with the way in which this was redefined, reworked indeed, around the Messiah and the Spirit, not least in the doctrine of justification. We shall then look more briefly at the way all this was rooted in a fresh reading of scripture, challenging to the surrounding paganism, and put into effect through Paul's actual apostolic work.

2. Election: Jewish Views of God's People

It has become something of a mantra that there were many Judaisms, plural, in Paul's day; but for there to be a plural there must be something singular, the theme on which they represent variations. In addition, there will always be questions about how well Paul knew and represented his own native Judaism, or, to put it another way, how representative the Judaism he described, and engaged with, may have been of the wider picture at the time. Recent attempts to suggest a more variegated attitude to the Law than was allowed for by E. P. Sanders in *Paul and Palestinian Judaism* are undoubtedly right to stress variety, and undoubtedly wrong to try to use that as a way of smuggling back an anachronistic vision of a Pelagian (or semi-Pelagian) or medieval works-righteousness. I shall be in implicit debate, in the detail of the exegesis and in the structure of thought, both with the so-called 'new perspective' and with its opponents; but I shall not have space for any hand-to-hand exchanges. My aim is a more strategic outflanking.[1]

The belief that Israel was the chosen people of the creator God is everywhere apparent in the Old Testament and the second-Temple literature, and indeed in all that we know of the praxis and symbolic world of both ancient Israel and first-century Judaism. The great stories which Israel told year by year were designed to celebrate and reinforce this status, often in the teeth of contrary evidence (oppression by pagan nations, corruption within Israel itself). We hardly need rehearse the stories of the patriarchs, the Exodus and conquest, the monarchy and its problems, the prophetic tradition of calling Israel back to its God, or the Psalms which simultaneously celebrated Israel's special status and lamented its failure to live up to its calling. All through it was a basic belief that the one creator God had called Israel to be his special people, and as part of that call had given Israel the land to live *in* and the Law to live *by*.

When Israel asked why it had been chosen, the answer came back, from Deuteronomy in particular, that it was purely a matter of God's love (7.8). But when Israel asked what purpose God had in mind in doing this, the ultimate answer came back in a variety of ways which were variously embraced, lost sight of, distorted and re-emphasized down the years. For the writer of Genesis, the call of Abraham was God's answer to the problem of Adam which had become the problem of Babel. Human rebellion had led to arrogance, pride and the fracturing of human life. The canonical Old Testament frames the entire story of God's people as the divine answer to the problem of evil: somehow, through this people, God will deal with the problem that has infected his good creation in general and his image-bearing creatures in particular. Israel is to be God's royal nation of holy priests, chosen out of the world but also for the sake of the world. Israel is to be the light of the world: the nations will see in Israel what it means to be truly human, and hence who the true God is. For this purpose, Israel is given Torah. As the psalmist remarks

(147.20), with a certain unappealing smugness, this makes Israel different from everybody else.

This whole theology of election is stated classically in the Exodus story, and reinforced by regular repetition and multiple subsequent allusions. It is put to the test in the events of exile, but again and again reaffirmed through that tragedy. The bearers of God's solution are themselves, declare the prophets, part of the problem; and as the Old Testament writers address this problem they find ways of declaring that YHWH will nevertheless fulfil both the original purpose *through* Israel and the contingent purpose *for* Israel.

All this was worked out in various ways in the second-Temple period. Worsening pagan oppression led to sundry reassertions of Israel's status as God's chosen people, to efforts to sustain and develop obedience to Torah, to attempts to purify the Land, not least by getting rid of pagan oppressors. Election was closely bound up with eschatology: because Israel was the one people of the one creator God, this God would soon act to vindicate Israel by liberating it from its enemies. Different writers drew the conclusion in different ways. Some documents, like the *Psalms of Solomon*, envisaged a fulfilment of Psalm 2, with Israel under its Messiah smashing the Gentiles to pieces with a rod of iron. Others, not least some of the rabbis in the Hillelite tradition, envisaged a redemption which, once it had happened to Israel, would then spread to the nations as well. Both of these represent natural developments of the doctrine of election itself, the point being that because Israel was the chosen people of the one creator God, when God did for Israel what God was going to do for Israel – however that was conceived – then the Gentiles would be brought into the picture, whether in judgment or blessing or (somehow) both. One way or another, God's purpose in election, to root evil out of the world and to do so through Israel, would be fulfilled.

So much for a summary which is too brief but already too long. We must hurry on to the central topic: Paul's exposition of the way in which, through Jesus and the Spirit, Israel's God had reshaped the doctrine of election itself.

3. Election Reshaped around Jesus

Paul reaffirmed Israel's election even at the moments when he was redefining it. Romans 9.4: 'They are Israel,' he writes, 'and to them belong the sonship, the glory, the covenants, the giving of the law, the worship, the promises, the patriarchs and the Messiah himself.' For Paul this is non-negotiable, and this is part of the glory and the puzzle of his theology. How much easier it would have been, both intellectually and politically, if, as many have imagined, Paul had constructed a theology in which Israel's election was either ignored, or overthrown, or left statically in place without redefinition! But Paul refuses: God will be true to his original promises though all humans, Israel included, are false (Romans 3.1–4). It is natural for him to go back to Abraham, as he does in both Galatians and Romans, not merely incidentally or in order to take on particular opponents, but because he really does reaffirm the election of Israel from the patriarchs onwards.

But election has also been redefined.[2] The obvious place to begin is Galatians, which I persist in seeing as very early. Certainly on this topic it is very clear.

In Galatians 2.11–21 Paul homes in on the crucial issue between him and Peter in Antioch: what does it mean, in practical terms, to be a member of God's people? The discussion only makes sense if we assume that the Christian community in Antioch has been living as in some sense the renewed Israel, and that they now face the question of whether or not uncircumcised Gentiles count within that company, or whether they belong at a separate table. Verses 14 and 15 indicate that the question, 'What does it mean to be a Jew?', lies behind the argument: 'If you,' Paul says to Peter, 'though you are a Jew, live in a Gentile fashion rather than a Jewish fashion, how can you force Gentiles to Judaize?' Peter, by separating himself from uncircumcised believers, is implying that if they want to belong to God's people they must take on themselves the identity of ethnic Jews by getting circumcised. There then follows the first ever statement of Paul's doctrine of justification by faith, and, despite the shrill chorus of detractors, it here obviously refers to *the way in which God's people have been redefined*. 'We', affirms Paul, 'are by birth Jews, not "gentile sinners"; yet we know that one is not justified by works of Torah, but through the faithfulness of Jesus the Messiah; thus we too have believed in the Messiah, Jesus, so that we might be justified by the faithfulness of the Messiah and not by works of Torah, because through works of Torah no flesh will be justified.'

There is enough there to keep us going all day, but let me simply spell out three points. First, I have translated *pistis Christou* and similar phrases as a reference, not to human *faith in* the Messiah but to the *faithfulness of* the Messiah, by which I understand, not Jesus' own 'faith' in the sense either of belief or trust, but his faith*fulness* to the divine plan for Israel. I mentioned this in an earlier chapter in connection with Romans 3, to which I shall return presently. Second, the passage works far better if we see the meaning of 'justified', not as a statement about how someone becomes a Christian, but as a statement about *who belongs to the people of God, and how you can tell that in the present.* That is the subject under discussion. Third, the point of 'works of Torah' here is not about the works some might think you have to perform in order to *become* a member of God's people, but the works you have to perform to *demonstrate that you are* a member of God's people. These works, Paul says, simply miss the point, as Psalm 143.2 had indicated, partly because nobody ever performs them adequately, and partly because, here and elsewhere, works of Torah would simply create a family which was at best an extension of ethnic Judaism, whereas God desires a family of all peoples, the point which is repeatedly emphasized in Galatians 3.

The rest of the paragraph spells out the results, highlighting the way this extraordinary redefinition of God's people has been effected through the Messiah, specifically through his death. Verses 17 and 18 face the question of what happens when 'we', or then 'I', find ourselves thus redefined. Does this make us technically 'sinners'? No, on the contrary, if we go back within the high protective walls erected by Torah around Israel, all we discover is that Torah itself declares us to be transgressors. There is a straight line from this point to Romans 7, where the 'I' of Galatians 2.18 has nearly a whole chapter to itself; but that must wait. What follows is central to Paul's messianic redefinition of election. Continuing with the 'I', which clearly refers not to Paul's private spiritual experience but to what happens to a Jew who believes in the Messiah, Paul declares that something has happened to this 'I'. 'I through Torah died to Torah, so that I might live to God.' This typically compressed statement needs a lot of unpacking, but basically it describes a dying and a coming to new life – resurrection itself, we note, being a major theme of an election-shaped eschatology in this period –

through which a new identity has emerged, the new identity which (we should never forget in reading the end of Galatians 2) underpins the stance Paul has taken in verses 11 to 16.

He then explains more specifically: 'I have been crucified with the Messiah; nevertheless I live; yet not I, but the Messiah lives in me; and the life I now live in the flesh, I live by faith in the Son of God who loved me and gave himself for me.' The elements of Paul's thought we studied earlier come together to explain his redefinition of election. The Messiah represents his people, so that what is true of him is true of them. He has been crucified; therefore they have been crucified with him (in Romans 6 Paul ties this to baptism, which may well be in mind here too). They now share his new life, not defined in terms of fleshly identity, that is, of Jewish ethnicity, but in terms of the Messiah's own new life, a life in which all nations can share equally. The energy driving this redefinition is nothing other than the love of the Messiah himself, just as in Deuteronomy the reason for election was simply the love of YHWH for Israel.

Paul then describes this in terms of grace. If he were to follow Peter and the others in rebuilding the wall separating Jews and Gentiles, he would be rejecting the grace of God. This final sentence is a cornerstone of a theologically reorientated version of the 'new perspective' on Paul: if righteousness, *dikaiosynē*, came by the Torah, then the Messiah died in vain. We note that here, in context, 'righteousness', *dikaiosynē*, must refer to *one's status as a member of God's people.* It means 'covenant status' or 'covenant membership'.[3] Paul is denying that this covenant status is defined by Torah – which it would still be if Peter and the others had their way. He is denying that Christians should separate for meals, with Jews at one table and uncircumcised Gentiles at the other. The doctrine of justification by faith was born into the world as the key doctrine underlying the *unity* of God's renewed people.

This is worked out in detail in the following chapter, where (as I have argued at length elsewhere[4]) the main theme is the fact that God has one family, not two, and that this family consists of all those who believe in the gospel. Faith, not the possession and/or practice of Torah, is the badge which marks out this family, the family which is now defined as the people of the Messiah. Galatians 3.23–29 spells this out in detail, taking the argument right back to Abraham where it began earlier in the chapter. Those who believe, those who are baptized into the Messiah, form the single family; they have come 'into the Messiah', they have 'put on the Messiah', they 'belong to the Messiah', they are 'in the Messiah'. And this single family, redefined around and by the Messiah, is the single family God promised to Abraham; that (3.29) is the punchline of the whole argument, showing once more what Paul's main purpose has been. God's people in the Messiah, we may note, are thereby marked out not simply against unbelieving Jews but, far more importantly, against the wider world of paganism. This redefinition of election is then rooted (as we saw in the previous chapter of the present book) in the redefinition of God himself as the son-sender and the Spirit-sender (4.1–7).

I skip to three verses almost at the end of the letter. In 6.14–16, Paul returns to what he has said in 2.11–21: the crucifixion of the Messiah means that everything has been turned inside out, not simply his own self, not simply Israel, but the entire cosmos. 'The world is crucified to me, and I to the world.' He thereby locates himself on the larger map of the purposes of God, which always stretched out *through* Israel to the restoration of the whole creation: 'what matters is neither circumcision nor uncircumcision but new creation'. From here there is a straight line both to 2 Corinthians 5 and, more especially, to Romans 8: Paul is not just speaking of the individual Christian as a new creation, though of course that is true as well, but of the entire renewal of the cosmos in which the Christian is invited to be a participant, in the sense both of beneficiary and of agent. And then, in true Jewish style, he invokes a blessing on those who walk according to this rule (as opposed to the rule of Torah): peace and mercy be on them, yes, even on God's Israel. In the light of the entire argument of the letter, I cannot agree with those who have pleaded that 'the Israel of God' in this verse denotes some subset of ethnic Judaism *over against* the people of God renewed in the Messiah. Paul has spent most of the letter explaining that God always intended to give Abraham a single family, and that he has now done so in the Messiah. It is special pleading, based shakily on a misreading of Romans 9—11, to suggest that 'God's Israel' here is anything other than the renewed family, the Messiah and his people. It is of course a polemical redefinition. Paul has saved it as a final, crucial point with which to round off the letter.

This points on to one of the other great passages where election is redefined: Philippians 3. The chapter begins, after the cryptic first verse, with several polemical redefinitions: watch out for the dogs, the workers of evil, the mutilation (*katatomē*, a contemptuous pun on *peritomē*, circumcision). This indicates where the line of thought is going: Israel is redefined, the covenant people have been radically redrawn, around the Messiah himself. *Hēmeis gar hē peritomē*: noting both the emphasis and the definite article, we translate: 'The circumcision? that's us!' Not, we note, the 'true' circumcision, simply 'the circumcision'. And the 'us' is defined as 'those who worship God in Spirit, who boast in the Messiah, Jesus, and put no confidence in the flesh', the flesh which, as we have seen before, is one of Paul's regular ways not only of denoting Israel 'according to the flesh' but of aligning that ethnic Israel with the corruptible flesh of humankind. This is where Paul's critique joins hands with the prophets. Israel is the bearer of the solution to the world's ills; but Israel has itself become part of the problem.

Paul then launches into his mini-autobiography. He had all the privileges and pride of status one could possibly want as a Jew. The crown of the list, in verse 6, was the status of *dikaiosynē*, covenant membership, defined by Torah: he didn't just possess Torah, he was *amemptos*, blameless, in his keeping of it. There follows a clear, if as usual dense, statement of redefinition around the Messiah. All this gain he counted as loss through the Messiah; in fact, he says, I count everything as loss because of the knowledge of the Messiah, Jesus my Lord, which goes far beyond everything else; because of him I threw away everything else as so much trash, so that I could gain the Messiah and be found in him, *not having a righteousness of my own, arising from Torah, but that which is through the faithfulness of the Messiah, the righteousness from God which is upon faith*, knowing him, sharing his sufferings, being conformed to his death, in the hope of the ultimate resurrection from the dead.

This spectacular passage far outstrips the space available to examine it. I have highlighted the multiple, almost obsessive, references to the Messiah in and through whom the redefinition has taken place. As in Galatians 2, all is focused on his dying and rising, which have brought God's people out from under Torah and any sense of being defined by it, and have given them instead a new covenant status, based on the achievement of the Messiah and bestowed upon those who now believe the gospel. We note particularly, because this is often misunderstood, that the status which Paul describes in verse 9 as belonging to those in the Messiah is not 'the righteousness of God', not God's *own* righteousness, but *hē ek theou dikaiosynē*, the covenant status which comes *from* God. This phrase is not a parallel, as is still often asserted, with *dikaiosynē theou* in Romans 10.3, though to be sure the two passages are closely related. The emphasis in Philippians 3 is not quite the same as in Galatians 2; for a start, there is more of a forward look, with the sharing of the Messiah's sufferings taking the place of the past crucifixion, and the ultimate hope of resurrection taking the place of the present resurrection life (not that these are in any way incompatible; it is simply a difference of emphasis). But again we note the way in which this redefinition of election is closely intertwined with the redefinition of God himself. Philippians 3, as has often been noted, is based squarely on Philippians 2.6–11.

With Galatians and Philippians behind us there are many other passages we could explore which fill in the picture. I have often been struck by the way in which, in 1 Corinthians 10.1, Paul addresses a largely Gentile church with the statement that 'our fathers' were all under the cloud and went through the sea. He doesn't need to explain; he can take it for granted that the family of God in Christ in Corinth simply *is* the family rescued by God from Egypt, now transformed and expanded, but still the same people. He contrasts this renewed family, later in the chapter, with 'Israel according to the flesh' (v. 18); and at the end of the chapter (v. 32) he urges the church not to give offence 'to Jews, or Greeks, or to the church of God'. Clearly the later idea of the church as a *tertium genus* has its roots in Paul himself, despite the attempts to protect him from it. We might also draw in, again with the usual caveats (and the usual cavalier disregard for normal scholarly prejudice), Ephesians 2 and 3, where the blood of the Messiah has brought Gentiles to the point where, having formerly been excluded from the covenant, they are now full and equal members of it. It is one of the telling features of current debate that some within the new perspective have, as it were, highlighted Ephesians 2.11–21, while most of the let's-go-back-to-the-old-perspective brigade have, as it were, highlighted 2.1–10. Clearly for either Paul or one of his first readers this was not an either/or, but a both/and. In any case, Ephesians 2.11—3.13 forms a lengthy and powerful statement of the redefinition of election around the Messiah – once again rooted in the redefinition of God himself, here (as we noted earlier) in the opening *berakah* of 1.3–11.

Having swallowed the camel of Ephesians, there is no need to strain out the gnat of Colossians, where chapter 2 provides another striking redefinition of election. You have already been circumcised, says Paul (v. 11); the Torah has nothing more to say to you, following the Messiah's cross (v. 14); you died and rose again, just as in Galatians 2 (2.20; 3.1), and you must let that redefined identity determine your path to holiness, rather than hoping to attain that goal by taking upon yourselves the regulations of Torah (2.16–23). In other words (v. 8), don't let anyone lead you away captive. But the word Paul uses for 'lead away captive', the very rare *sylagōgōn*, seems, like the equivalent words in Philippians 3, to be a contemptuous pun. All you have to do is invert the lambda (in cursive writing) or add a stroke to it (in capitals) and you get *synagōgōn*: συλαγωγων/συναγωγων; ΣΥΛΑΓΩΓΩΝ/ΣΥΝΑΓΩΓΩΝ; in other words, 'don't let anyone en-synagogue you, drag you into the synagogue'. And this redefinition of election in Colossians 2 and 3 is once more based foursquare on the redefinition of monotheism, already described, in Colossians 1.

But it is of course with Romans that the redefinition of God's people around the Messiah reaches its full height. I have said a good deal about Romans already in this book (as well as my two commentaries and various articles), and there is more to come; but our present theme demands a further trawl through with our eye on this particular topic. At some points we shall inevitably anticipate my second category, the redefinition around the Spirit, so that this segment forms a kind of transition to the second part of the chapter.

We begin in Romans 2. Having denounced human idolatry and sin in 1.18—2.16, Paul turns his attention to his own former self and those who still think as he did prior to his conversion. Verses 17–25 examine the Jewish claim to special status, based on election and the covenant; the prophets themselves find these claims undermined by Israel's sin. Paul is not here talking about every individual Jew, as is regularly supposed, but about the *national* boast which declares that ethnic Israel as a whole remains inviolate. Instead of being the light of the world, Israel has caused the pagan nations to blaspheme. Boasting in Torah is rendered null and void by breaking Torah. The presence of sin within Israel destroys the claim that Israel, as it stands, is the people through whom God will accomplish his purposes in the world.

The next paragraph lies very close to Philippians 3.2–3 in its dramatic redefinition of what it means to be circumcised. The theme of circumcision of the heart goes back through various second-Temple passages to Jeremiah, Deuteronomy and elsewhere, and Paul here exploits it fully. Supposing, he muses, God has created a category of people who, though uncircumcised, keep the Torah (an oxymoron only matched by 1 Corinthians 7.19: neither circumcision nor uncircumcision matters, since what matters is keeping God's commands!), and who will in fact sit in judgment on those who, though circumcised and possessing the Torah, nevertheless break it. The last two verses of the chapter (2.28–29) are the key, though their dense Greek almost defies translation, and they depend for their force on another pun, this time a hidden one. The Hebrew for 'praise' is *jehuda*, 'Judah', so that the very name 'Jew', *Ioudaios* in Greek, ought to mean 'praise'. This highlights what Paul is saying: the very word *Ioudaios* is now to be predicated of a different group, no longer defined ethnically or by the possession of Torah, not marked out by things which are *en tō phanerō*, 'in the open' or 'on the surface'. Rather, *ho en tō kryptō Ioudaios*, 'the Jew in secret', that is, 'the Jew is the Jew who is so in secret', and 'circumcision' consists in the spirit rather than the letter. Such a person, Paul declares with the Hebrew in mind, gains 'praise' not from humans but from God. We note, as in Philippians 3, that Paul does not say 'the true Jew' or 'the real circumcision', however much we are tempted to add such extra words both to make the meaning easier to appropriate and to cushion our sensibilities against the blunt, clear claim.

The Messiah has not been mentioned so far in this part of Romans. The passage we have just studied belongs properly, as I said, with the redefinition of election through the Spirit. But we need those verses as the backdrop to what happens next, in a passage as vital for Romans and Pauline theology as it is routinely neglected, namely 3.1–9. This is all about the election of Israel, the way in which Israel's faithlessness has threatened God's elective purpose, and the solution which God has found. Paul's point is precisely that, in the Messiah, God has remained faithful to the purpose of election despite Israel's faithlessness.

The key is to recognize that in 3.2 and 3.3 the point of Israel's call to be faithful is that election was never about Israel being called for its own sake, but always about God's call of Israel to be the light of the world. This, indeed, seems itself to be part of Paul's retelling of the story; not all Jews of his day, I think, might so readily have seen Israel as essentially existing for some larger purpose. No, he says, Israel was *entrusted* with God's oracles; that is, Israel was cast, within God's cosmic drama, as the messenger through whose faithful work the creator would bring the news of his power and love to the whole world. The question of some being unfaithful (v. 3) does not mean that Israel has not 'had faith' in the sense of believing in God or his purpose, though that may be so as well; the point is that Israel has been unfaithful *to the commission God had given it.* Paul, we may note, could only think and write like this if, as I have insisted, he believed that God had chosen Israel and had not rescinded that choice. What then is to happen? 'Let God be true, though all humans are false': God will keep to his plan, *to save the world through Israel,* even though the chosen people are now bound up in the problem instead of being the bringers of the solution.

But how will God do this? How, granted universal human sin, will God be faithful to the covenant with Israel, and faithful to the purpose, through the covenant, for the world? How will God keep the promises he made to Abraham and his family? If, as part of the terms of that covenant, Israel is to be the means of God addressing and dealing with the problem of evil, how, granted Israel's faithlessness, can the plan of election go ahead? This, all together, is the problem of the *dikaiosynē theou*, the righteousness of God. It is to this precise problem, not simply that of universal human sin, that Romans 3.21–26 is addressed, in another typically dense yet powerfully programmatic pronouncement. And at its heart we discover, as the following verses (27–31) indicate, that Paul is once more redefining, around the Messiah, what it means to be the people of God.

God's covenant faithfulness is revealed, through the faithfulness of the Messiah, for the benefit of all who believe, Jew and Gentile alike. That is the point of 3.21–26. This is my primary reason for understanding *pistis Christou*, in other passages as well, as referring in shorthand form to the Messiah's faithfulness to God's plan rather than to human belief or trust in the Messiah, though of course that remains important as well; the two are closely correlated. And the point about the Messiah's faithfulness is that it is another way of referring to the Messiah's *obedience*, as in Romans 5.12–21 and Philippians 2.8, a way of denoting the same thing while *con*noting that faithfulness which was required under God's covenant plan. And as soon as we ask what this faithfulness, this obedience, consisted in, Philippians 2 and the whole of Romans 1—8 give the answer: it was the Messiah's sacrificial death. This is at the heart of the redefinition of election around the Messiah: that through his death, explored from all kinds of angles in this letter and elsewhere, God's purpose, to rescue the world from the entail of sin and death, has at last been accomplished. The Messiah has done that for which Israel was chosen in the first place. His death, described densely in the present passage, has made the atonement through which all nations are redeemed. God's faithfulness is therefore fully and finally unveiled in the cross. The Messiah has done for the world what Israel was called to do. He has done *in Israel's place* what Israel was called to do but could not, namely to act on behalf of the whole world. God has set him forth as a *hilastērion*. All those who believe the gospel message of his death and resurrection are now themselves accorded the status of *dikaios*: righteous, forgiven, within the covenant. Here as elsewhere (as I suggested in the previous chapter) the cross of the Messiah lies at the centre of Paul's reworking of election, of God's people.

This passage, and particularly verses 27–31 which follow, show how impossible it is therefore to separate the doctrine of justification by faith from that of the incorporation of Gentiles into the people of God. The attempt to do so can only even begin by screening out the larger theology in which Paul fully shares and shrinking the whole argument to nothing but an individualistic, ahistoricized and de-covenantalized parody. (I have recently seen apparently serious attempts to arrive at such a position by pretending that the paragraph ends at verse 28, whereas close attention to the words Paul uses, particularly the connecting *ē*, 'or', at the start of verse 29, indicates that verses 29–31 are an integral and indeed climactic part of his train of thought.) A person, concludes Paul, is justified by faith apart from works of Torah: that is, the only badge of membership in

God's people is the badge of faith, faith which is open to all, Jew and Gentile alike – otherwise God would seem to be God only of Jews, not of Gentiles also, as would inevitably be the case if Torah, the Law given only to Jews, were the means or standard of definition. And, once again, the redefinition of election is rooted in Paul's Jewish theology of the one God: 'yes, of Gentiles also, since God is one'. This then leads directly into Romans 4, which is itself a major redefinition of election, expounding Genesis 15 to show that the inclusion of Gentiles had always been God's will and purpose, and that, from Abraham all the way through to the present, the defining characteristic of God's true people had been faith in God as the creator and life-giver, the faith now shared by those who believe in the God who raised Jesus from the dead (4.18–25).

How then does 'justification by faith' actually work? I sketched this towards the end of the third chapter, and I now want to fill it in a bit more. Paul has already spoken in Romans 2 about the final justification of God's people, on the basis of their whole life. This will take place at the end, when God judges the secrets of all hearts through the Messiah. The point of justification *by faith* is that, as he insists in 3.26, it takes place *in the present time* as opposed to on the last day. It has to do with the questions, 'Who now belongs to God's people?', and 'How can you tell?' The answer is: all who believe in the gospel belong, and that is the only way you can tell – not by who their parents were, or how well they have obeyed the Torah (or any other moral code), or whether they have been circumcised. *Justification, for Paul, is a subset of election*, that is, it belongs as part of his doctrine of the people of God.

And of course this does *not* mean, despite many efforts to push the conclusion this way, that it has nothing to do with sinners being saved from sin and death by the love and grace of God. The point of election always was that humans were sinful, that the world was lapsing back into chaos, and that God was going to mount a rescue operation. That is what the covenant was designed to do, and that is why 'belonging to the covenant' means, among other things, 'forgiven sinner'. The point is that the *word* 'justification' does not itself *denote* the process whereby, or the event in which, a person is brought by grace from unbelief, idolatry and sin into faith, true worship and renewal of life. Paul, clearly and unambiguously, uses a different word for that, the word 'call'. The word 'justification', despite centuries of Christian misuse, is used by Paul to denote that which happens immediately after the 'call': 'those God called, he also justified' (Romans 8.30). In other words, those who hear the gospel and respond to it in faith are *then* declared by God to be his people, his elect, 'the circumcision', 'the Jews', 'the Israel of God'. They are given the status *dikaios*, 'righteous', 'within the covenant'.

But the word 'call' itself, and the fact that 'justification' is not about 'how I get saved' but 'how I am declared to be a member of God's people', must always have an eye to the larger purposes of the covenant. Indeed, to forget this, as has often been done within western theology both Catholic and Protestant, is to make a mistake not too unlike that for which Paul chides his fellow countrymen. The point of the covenant was to deal with idolatry and sin in order that the world as a whole could be rescued – and there is no question, once we read Romans 5—8, that that is where Paul intends his argument to go. Thus the point of human beings being called by the gospel to turn from idolatry and sin to worship the true and living God is *both* that they might themselves be rescued *and* that through their rescue, and the new community which they then form, God's purposes to rescue the whole world might be advanced. This is why, in Romans 5.17, Paul speaks of the justified 'reigning in life'; the aim is not simply that they should themselves be rescued from disaster, but that through them God would rule his new creation. And this is why, too, the coming together of Jews and Gentiles in the one family is so central to justification. It is not simply about making life easier for Gentile converts who might not like the thought of circumcision, as some have said in trying to pour scorn on the 'new perspective'. It is, as Ephesians 3 saw so gloriously, that through this creation of a Jew-plus-Gentile family the living God might declare to the principalities and powers that their time is up, and might launch the whole project of new creation. The rethinking of election around the Messiah, and its reworking by Paul in his apostolic labours to generate and sustain exactly this kind of community, holds together elements of his thought which centuries of alternative systems have forced apart.

I leave to one side for the moment the greatest passage of all on the redefinition of election, and pass rapidly to the second main segment of this chapter, the redefinition of election around the Spirit.

4. Election Reworked around the Spirit

We have already noticed that in one key passage in Romans, 2.25–29, Paul has hinted strongly at a redefinition of election which takes place 'in the spirit not the letter'. As we saw in the previous chapter, this is worked out in Romans 8 in particular, where it is the Spirit who leads the renewed people through the wilderness to their inheritance – or, to put it another way, it is the Spirit who enables them to put to death the deeds of the body and so to live that genuinely human existence which is what Torah longed to produce but could not. This is also a major theme, of course, in Galatians 5. But when we look outwards from Romans 2, and indeed Philippians 3, we see one spectacular passage in which this redefinition of election by the Spirit is spelled out fully, namely 2 Corinthians 3.

The problems that this passage has presented to interpreters are resolved if we remind ourselves frequently that the contrast at its heart is not between the Law itself and the gospel, not between Moses and Jesus, but between the *hearers* of Moses and those who believe in Jesus. Torah was given, Paul says, to people with hard hearts and darkened minds. As a result, they were not able to look at the glory of God revealed on Moses' face. But where the Spirit of the Lord is, there the apostle and his congregation can look one another in the face, can stare at the glory there revealed, and can by this means be transformed from one degree of glory to another. All this is based on the most explicit 'covenant renewal' passage in Paul, namely 3.1–6, a passage closely cognate both with Romans 2.25–29 and with Romans 7.4–6 (about which more in a moment).

'God has qualified us', says Paul, 'to be ministers of the new covenant, not in the letter but in the Spirit, because the letter kills, but the Spirit gives life' (v. 6). The main subject of the whole passage, through to the middle of chapter 6, is Paul's apostolic ministry and the vindication of its style and content over against the criticisms of those who wanted it to be more obviously glorious, more spectacular. But part of the point is that the Corinthians ought to be able to receive his ministry, precisely because they, too, have had the Spirit at work in their hearts (v. 3) through Paul's preaching of the gospel. They are therefore the beneficiaries of, the members of, God's renewed covenant; Paul here draws on two passages he alludes to in several other places, namely Ezekiel 36 and Jeremiah 31. A new dispensation has come about, in which condemnation and death are being replaced by vindication and righteousness; and these now belong to the people who are being renewed by the Spirit.

This sends us back to Romans 7, where the same theme is apparent though without the explicit mention of covenant renewal. Here the themes we have seen in Galatians 2 and 2 Corinthians 3 come together: 'you died to the law through the body of the Messiah, so that you could belong to another, the one who was raised from the dead . . . so that you might serve in the newness of the spirit and not the oldness of the letter' (7.4–6). This is then picked up in Romans 8.5–8, where again Paul uses language replete with the overtones of covenant renewal to speak of God's people as being redefined by 'the law of the Spirit of life in the Messiah, Jesus'.

To this category (the reworking of election by the Spirit) belong those twin themes of 1 Corinthians and elsewhere, the renewed temple and the body of the Messiah. The passages in chapters 3 and 6 about the new Temple, where God now dwells by the Spirit, speak of the presence of Israel's God in and with his people; only now it is a people composed of human beings from all kinds of backgrounds. The picture of the Messiah's body is not introduced in chapter 12 merely in order to provide a convenient illustration of unity and diversity, but in order to make a powerful statement about the renewed people as precisely God's new humanity – that which Israel was called to be but failed to be.

The major theme which marks out Paul's theology of God's people as renewed through the Spirit is the renewed call to holiness. It is a holiness not defined by Torah, and yet in much of what Paul says he can draw upon Torah for outline guidance in ways which have been studied in detail by those better qualified than I.[5] It is, as the prophets always wanted, a holiness which comes from the heart; and it is a holiness which ought to make the pagan nations see who the living God really is. It is, in other words, not simply a matter of 'now you are saved, this is how to behave'; it is a matter of the genuine humanness envisaged as God's will for Israel being attained through the Spirit by God's renewed people. It is summed up well at the start of Romans 12, in the appeal for self-offering and transformation through the renewal of the mind, resulting in the mutual upbuilding of those who, though many, are one body in the Messiah. What we have here, in fact, is the explicit undoing and reversal of the decline and decay of humanness outlined in 1.18–32; in other words, those in the Messiah and transformed by the Spirit are to be that which Israel was called to be. There is much more to say about how Paul reconfigures election by the Spirit, but this should serve to point in the right direction.

5. Redefinition of Election Rooted in Scripture

I have left until now, and perhaps too late in this chapter, the most remarkable sustained argument anywhere in Paul, which is his treatment of the problem of Israel in Romans 9—11.

Among other reasons for considering it remarkable is the way in which the Messiah is hardly mentioned (9.5 and 10.4–13), and the Spirit not at all after the opening remark about Paul's conscience bearing him witness in the Spirit that he has unceasing grief in his heart. Some have suggested that this is because Paul is trying to find a way of affirming the forward pathway of unbelieving Israel independent of the Messiah and the Spirit.[6] I think this is quite wrong. It is straightforwardly disproved by 10.4–13, which I expounded in the previous chapter and which occupies a central place in the section. There it is clear that Paul believes that the events concerning Jesus are the fulfilment of the promises in Deuteronomy 30, and that those who wish to be part of the covenant renewal spoken of in that passage – the return from exile, no less – must come to faith in the Messiah. His quotation of Joel in 10.13 indicates, at least to those able to decode such echoes, that a theology of the Spirit is strongly implied here as well; in other words, that in this section Paul is drawing on the themes he has set out earlier in the letter. If anything, I think the apparent reticence of the section has more to do with tactics. Paul wants to enable the Roman church to think the whole thing through from the first principles embodied in scripture itself.

Romans 9—11 is, in fact, a massive retelling of the scriptural narrative, on a par in its way with the remarkable retelling in the second half of the Wisdom of Solomon and other similar second-Temple narratival passages. The point throughout 9.6–29 is that what has happened to Israel is what God always intended. As Paul thinks his way through the story of the patriarchs, the Exodus and the time of the prophets, it is clear that God never intended Israel to be affirmed as it stood. God had, it seems, called Abraham and his family to be the solution-bearing family knowing that, because they too were 'in Adam', they were themselves bound to become part of the problem, and that the shape of their own history was thus bound to bear witness to their own share in the problem whose solution they were none the less carrying. This line of thought reaches its height at the start of chapter 10, where, just as in 3.21, the Messiah himself reveals what God's covenant plan had been all along. But as the argument of chapter 10 works through to the statement of Paul's missionary policy in verses 14–18, it leaves him still with the puzzle: if God has, as he promised, made Israel jealous by bringing in Gentiles to share the covenant privileges, what is now to happen to 'Israel according to the flesh'?

It is at this point, of course, that many have tried to mount an exegetical argument to say that, while Paul has indeed explained the renewal of the covenant, the rethinking of election, as I have expounded it above, he here offers a different argument, supremely in 11.25–26, for thinking that God is also providing a special way of salvation, still reserved for Jews and Jews only. Indeed, not to mount such an argument is to run the risk of being accused of that current heresy, 'supersessionism', the mere mention of which is enough to drive otherwise clear-headed exegetes into abject apology and hasty backtracking. Has Paul really so redefined election around Messiah and Spirit that there is no room for anyone who clings to the original election while rejecting those two redefining poles? Is not Paul's whole argument in chapter 11 that, despite their unbelief, the Jewish people are still 'beloved because of the patriarchs' (v. 28)?

Yes, but this does not mean what the revisionist argument tries to make it mean. As I have argued in considerable detail elsewhere, the promise Paul holds out for at present unbelieving Jews is not that they are actually all right as they are, but *that they are not debarred, in virtue of their ethnic origin*, from coming back into the family, their own family, that has been renewed in the gospel, and from which they are currently separated because it is marked out solely by faith, and they are currently in 'unbelief'. Romans 10.1–13 remains, in fact, a crucial driver of the argument right through chapter 11, as the various links between the two passages (not often enough noted) indicate; in particular, when Paul says 'all Israel shall be saved' in 11.26 he is consciously echoing 'all who call on the name of the Lord shall be saved' in 10.13, which is offered as the answer to the question of 10.1 about the salvation for presently unbelieving Jews. As he says in 11.23, they can be grafted in *if they do not remain in unbelief.* Had he held the views normally attributed to him, he could not have written that line.[7]

Paul's argument is not aimed at our modern western context, in which centuries of horrible European anti-Semitism have finally worked their way out in an orgy of violence, implicating many parts of the Christian church. His argument is aimed at the proto-Marcionism he suspects may exist in the Roman church, an attitude which really would deserve the name 'supersessionism', a belief according to which God has effected a simple transfer of promises and privileges from Jews to Gentiles, so that Jews are just as shut out now as Gentiles were before (a very convenient thing to believe in Rome in the middle or late 50s after those unpopular Jews were allowed back again upon Nero's accession). This argument has nothing to do, either, with the idea, which neither Paul nor his contemporaries would have understood, since it belongs primarily with the eighteenth-century European Enlightenment, that each religion is more or less as good as each other one, and that Judaism and Christianity are parallel ways of believing in the one God and should each learn to shrug their shoulders and go their separate ways. That, for Paul, would paradoxically have been the ultimate form of anti-Judaism – the idea that the Jews should be encouraged to ignore their own Messiah, to sidestep the renewal of their own covenant, and to remain in ignorance of the *dikaiosynē theou*, of what the creator God had righteously been doing in Israel's own history.

Rather, Romans 9—11 as a whole, though it does not say very much about Messiah and Spirit, is in fact *shaped* according to the pattern which Paul elsewhere works out very explicitly in those terms. It is as though, soaked in the thought expressed in Galatians 2.11–21 and similar passages explored above, he were to set himself the task of thinking through what it means that, as he says in 9.5, the Messiah is Israel's Messiah according to the flesh and also 'God over all, blessed for ever'. What we see worked out in 9—11, in other words, is the Messiah-shaped pattern of Israel's history, with the Spirit-driven pathway to covenant renewal blazed through the middle of it. As in 11.11–15, Israel itself is 'cast away' for the reconciliation of the world, and thus can and will be 'received back again' with a meaning of nothing short of 'life from the dead'. Paul has so retold the story of Israel according to the Messianic pattern worked out earlier in the letter that, when we stand back and look at the picture as a whole, what strikes us is not the relative absence of Messiah and Spirit but the fact that the whole of Israel's story is laid before us as the outworking in history of what it means that, as the fulfilment of God's promises to Abraham, the Messiah was crucified and raised to new life.

6. Conclusion

Each element of the present chapter, but especially the last one, has highlighted the multiple ways in which Paul's reworking of the Jewish doctrine of election necessarily involved him in fresh readings of scripture, readings which stand beside and in implicit dialogue with other readings of the same scriptures in roughly the same period. We must just glance, in conclusion, at the other two constant themes which slice through Paul's reworking of the three central Jewish doctrines.

As we would expect, Paul's reworking of election, since it remains a redefinition and not an abandonment of the Jewish belief, solidifies his stance over against paganism. This is of course counter-intuitive to an entire strand of Pauline study, which has hailed Paul as the religious hero who broke loose from Judaism and invented Christianity as a new form of non-Jewish religion. Paul would have been horrified by such an idea – which, again, would represent the real 'supersessionism'. Rather, the communities which spring up where he has announced the gospel are to order their lives as those who look back to Abraham, to the Exodus, to the Law (in its true fulfilment), to the prophets; and at each point this means, as those who stand out as children of light amidst the world of darkness.[8] And, since one of the main manifestations of paganism in Paul's world, as in the Old Testament, is the power of pagan empire, we return for a moment to Chapter 4 above: through the church, specifically in its reworked-election existence as the single people from all nations, God's many-splendoured wisdom is to be made known to the principalities and powers in the heavenly places.

This is where we can see, too, how Paul's actual praxis embodies the reworked election we have been studying. Paul's whole ministry is shaped by this reworking: he is constantly labouring to produce and maintain cells of Jews and Gentiles loyal to Jesus as Messiah and Lord, living in the power of the Spirit, under the nose of Caesar and in some of the key cities of the empire. That might lead us to wonder what sort of agendas, not only in ecclesiology but also in politics, Paul would want to urge on us today – a question to which I hope to return briefly in the final chapter. But our more immediate task, to which we now turn, is to put together Paul's rethinking of God and his reworking of God's people, and to show how together they generate and sustain the vital third element in his very Jewish theology: reimagining God's future.

7

Reimagining God's Future

1. Introduction

We come now to the third part of Paul's rethinking and reworking of traditional Jewish theology. As in the previous chapter, I have changed my original title ('rethinking') for something more appropriate, in this case 'reimagining', since part of Paul's task, in teaching the Christian hope to puzzled converts, was precisely to educate their imagination, to lift their eyes beyond the small horizons of their previous worldviews.

As I explained in the last two chapters, within a good deal of Jewish thought of the period there was a clear undercurrent running from the two primary topics (monotheism, election) to the third (eschatology). If there is one God, and if this God is the God of Israel, then – granted the present state of the world, and of Israel – this God must act in the future to put things to rights. If he doesn't, then creation and covenant, monotheism and election, are themselves called in question. Eschatology, the question of God's future – not only of the future which God has in store for the world but (if we dare put it this way, as I think many Jewish thinkers would), the question of God's own future – is up for grabs. It is perhaps significant that death-of-God theology emerged in the twentieth century, albeit with roots in the nineteenth, precisely out of a world in which things had got so bad that it seemed not only that God could do nothing about it but also that God's very existence had been called into question. Reflections like this are not, it seems to me, simply the projection of our own postmodern angst back into the first century. Paul's greatest letter was itself not only an exposition of God's justice but a vindication of it, a demonstration that, once you reimagine the Jewish doctrine of eschatology around the Messiah and the Spirit, you glimpse not just God's future for the world, but God's future, full stop.

But this is to run ahead of the argument. Let us take things, as before, step by step. First we must give a brief, and necessarily tendentious, sketch of first-century Jewish eschatology. Then I shall try to show, through key exegetical examples and arguments, the way in which Paul redefined this eschatology around the Messiah and the Spirit. As I do so I shall note the ways in which this redefinition, itself rooted in Paul's re-reading of the Jewish scriptures, was making a claim over against the other Jewish claims of his time; the ways in which, like all Jewish eschatology from early in scripture to the present day, a claim was also being made over against the world of paganism; and the ways in which it worked out in Paul's actual praxis.

2. Jewish Eschatology in the First Century

To see the ways in which Jewish eschatology sets itself over against paganism, you only have to glance through books like Second Isaiah or Daniel. Israel's God is the one and only God, and he is both capable of, and committed to, acting in the future to defeat the pagan idols and their devotees. When he does, this will of course constitute new creation. The myrtle will come up in place of the briar, the cypress instead of the thorn; in other words, Genesis 3 will be reversed, as God's word comes from heaven to recreate the earth.[1] The Human One will be exalted over the beasts; in other words, Genesis 2 is to come true on a cosmic and global scale, establishing God's sovereignty, through faithful Israel, over the whole world.[2]

Into this picture we could (uncontroversially) factor literally dozens of key passages from prophets and psalms, passages which were often reused in the second-Temple period. God had plenty of quarrels to pick with Israel itself, but at the end of the day it was with the wickedness of the pagan world, and the dark forces that stood behind it, that he was principally concerned. Jeremiah has a great deal to say about Israel's wickedness and God's judgment upon it, but at the end of the book, as we saw earlier, it is Babylon that comes in for the greatest condemnation. There would come a Day of YHWH, a Day on which YHWH, as the creator and covenant God, would judge the whole world.

Of course, some prophets could and did turn the telescope around the other way. One of the earliest, Amos, takes an existing Day of

YHWH theme in which Israel expounds a standard anti-pagan eschatology, and turns it back on Israel itself: Why do you desire the Day of YHWH? It is a day of darkness, not light.[3] The Day will turn its spotlight on all, Israel included, and Israel's privileges will then form part of the accusation, not part of the speech for the defence. The prophets of the so-called post-exilic period live with the paradox that Israel seems both to be redeemed and emphatically not redeemed. They are back in their own land, but YHWH has not yet come back to the Temple. Malachi, faced with corruption in both priests and people, declares that he will indeed do so, suddenly and with ferocious force and effect.[4] Granted all that has happened, the only way forward now into YHWH's new world will be by his shaking the heavens and the earth, the sea and the dry land: Haggai looks back to Genesis 1 and imagines an earthquake shaking the entire cosmos, out of which there would emerge a world put to rights, a purified Israel, a glorious Jerusalem and Temple, and a true Davidic king who would be like the signet ring on YHWH's finger, the one (that is) in whose features Israel may trace the very stamp of God's presence.[5]

These themes – coming judgment, vindication of Israel, the Day of YHWH, the establishment of God's kingdom, the overthrow of paganism, the arrival of the Messiah, and so on – are all of course developed and highlighted, in numerous different ways, in the post-biblical second-Temple period. I have elsewhere argued at length, and still fail to see why this should be difficult to understand or establish, that the majority of Jews of this period for whom we have evidence understood the time in which they were living as a long story still in search of an ending, and that this story was often thematized as one of continuing exile, despite geographical return.[6] The word 'exile' is of course here being used metaphorically, but it is both a convenient, and theologically and biblically accurate, word to denote the perception of many, if not most, Jews of the time. Two texts are crucial for this perception, texts whose reuse and appropriation in the post-biblical period gives us important clues to the viewpoints of the time: Deuteronomy 30 and Daniel 9.

As we saw briefly in Chapter 6, Deuteronomy 30 forms part of a longer narrative about the blessings and the curses of the covenant. It is important to stress that it is a *narrative*, a story about a long historical sequence of events which will come upon Israel: first blessing, if Israel keeps the commandments, then curses if Israel does not – and the final, ultimate curse is exile. Then, in exile, Israel will turn back to YHWH with a whole heart, and YHWH will restore Israel's fortunes. The fact that this text was being used as a way of understanding where Israel still was in the last centuries BC indicates well enough that for those Jews at least the real exile, the oppression of Israel by the pagan nations, was not yet over, even if geographically some of them had returned from Babylon and had rebuilt the Temple. Only Ben-Sirach stands out as a clear counter-example to this narrative: The High Priest's in his Temple, says Ben-Sirach 50, all's right with the world (a position soon to be shattered by the Maccabean crisis and its aftermath). One might also cite Philo; but then he is an exception to a great many things, and in fact his own coded political messages may indicate that there was more contemporary narrative history to his exegesis than has often met the eye. In the post-exilic biblical books themselves there is a strong sense that, paradoxically, exile is not yet over after all. We are still slaves, declare Ezra and Nehemiah, even though we are in our own land.[7] And what slaves need is of course an Exodus.

We shall come to that in a moment, but we must just note as well both the fact of Daniel 9 and the strong probability that it was a very popular text in the first century. In the fictive scene of Daniel 9, the prophet, still in Babylon, enquires of God how long the exile is to go on for. Jeremiah had said it would last for seventy years; when will this time be up, this sentence be worked off?[8] The reply Daniel gets is hardly encouraging for someone during the actual Babylonian exile, but it was to prove not just encouraging but exciting for people in the last two centuries BC and the first two centuries AD. The exile will last, Daniel is told, not for seventy years but for *seventy weeks of years*; that is, seventy times seven, a kind of ultra-jubilee.[9] And there follows a cryptic prophecy about how the end would then come, through the work of an anointed prince, through the destruction of Jerusalem, the appearance of the abomination of desolation and the outpouring of great and terrible wrath. We know from several sources that this text was probed extensively for hints both of when precisely the great redemption – seen, we emphasize, as the ultimate return from exile – was going to happen, and of what these events would actually look like on the ground. This was a text, I have argued elsewhere, to which Jesus made potent if cryptic reference.

And this was the text, I believe, to which Josephus refers when he says that 'an oracle in their scriptures' drove the Jews pell-mell towards the revolution which broke out in the mid-60s AD.[10] Once we put Daniel 9 alongside the many texts which speak of a coming great battle, we discover a clear line not only into the theory of holy revolution (as expressed, for instance, in the War Scroll), but into its actual practice. Or, when we redefine it in the shocking way done by Jesus of Nazareth, into the road to Calvary.

My underlying point is this, drawing together what I said in the second and third chapters of this book. When first-century Jews thought of God's future, of a coming 'end' of whatever sort, they saw this *not* simply as a bolt from the blue, descending into an otherwise undifferentiated and irrelevant historical sequence. They saw it precisely as the climax, the denouement, of a story, a plot which had been steadily unfolding both in the mind of God and on the ground in the Middle East. The sharp line that used to be drawn between 'prophecy' and 'apocalyptic' bears witness to a grain of truth and a large heap of misunderstanding. This is among many lessons we ought to learn from Qumran, but it should actually have been clear to us from texts we knew already even before the Scrolls were discovered.

The end of slavery, as I said, was of course conceived in terms of a new Exodus. This is a major and familiar theme, but it needs drawing out a stage further. Imagery from the Exodus narrative was already being employed as a way of talking about the coming redemption in the great prophets and the psalms: Where is the God who divided the Red Sea into two? The God who earlier led his people through the wilderness will lead them home from Babylon. The God who breathed fire and smoke on Sinai would do the same again, to scatter his enemies and rescue Israel. Sometimes, as in the Wisdom of Solomon, the whole story, rooted in the creation stories and the patriarchal narratives, is retold with great power: this is how God in his wisdom acted to deliver his people from the pagan idolaters. And the reason for telling this story was of course far from being purely antiquarian, or for that matter purely about celebrating the wisdom of the God who did such powerful things. The point is that *God will do them again*. Within the larger single narrative, certain patterns will repeat, above all this one. The Exodus will happen again, on an even grander scale. Pagan rulers, be warned! And, while we're about it, Israel, be comforted! That is the underlying message of the Wisdom of Solomon.

Israel's ultimate comfort, of course, will come through the return of YHWH himself. He will suddenly come to his Temple, not only for judgment – important though that will be – but to save his people and, at last, bless them once more with his presence. I have written about this theme at length elsewhere and just need to mention it as an important part of Jewish eschatology and one which Paul, as with everything else, rethinks and – since this involves looking ahead to the future – reimagines.[11]

'Day of YHWH', 'Kingdom of God', victory over evil and pagan rulers, rescue of Israel, end of exile, the coming of the Messiah, the new Exodus, and the return of YHWH himself; and, in and through all of this, the resurrection of the dead. This is the combination of themes which characterizes the first-century Jewish expectation of the future. And, as I noted earlier, this is to be *God's* future in the sense that in this way God will come, so to speak, into his own. He will become King in a new way: 'On that day,' as the prophet puts it, 'YHWH will be king of all the earth, he will be one and his name one,' presumably in a way which somehow, strangely, is not yet true.[12] *How* this was to happen, what it would mean in practice, remained for many a mystery, a puzzle. *That* this eschatology would come to pass was a fundamental first-century Jewish belief, the inescapable corollary of monotheism and election.

3. Eschatology Reimagined around the Messiah

That all this has now come to pass in Jesus the Messiah is a central plank in the theology of St Paul. Cognate, and closely interwoven, with his redefinitions of monotheism and election, Paul's eschatology remains deeply Jewish in its shape and emphasis, right down to fresh retellings of the same narratives and fresh exegesis of some of the same key texts. Through his high Christology, it is indeed *God's own* future that has burst into the present. Through his incorporative Christology, summing up his redefined doctrine of election, it is *Israel's* future that has at last come to pass. Through his extraordinary interpretation of Jesus' crucifixion as the divine victory over the powers of evil, the great battle has come and gone, and the pagan powers have been decisively defeated. This is perhaps the first and most important thing to say about Paul's reworking of eschatology: that the complex event for which Israel had hoped had already happened in the events of Jesus of Nazareth. Jesus' resurrection indicated not just *that* something extraordinary had come to pass, but *what that extraordinary thing was*: the anticipation, breaking in to the scene of ongoing history, of the ultimate End. Inaugurated eschatology, framed, explained and given depth by the reworking of monotheism and election, is one of the most central and characteristic notes of Paul's whole theology. The still-future events of which he frequently speaks are themselves reworkings of the same Jewish expectations. And the creative tension between the two, between what has already happened in the Messiah and what is still to happen at the ultimate end, is where we must locate some of his most characteristic themes (justification, the body of Christ, and so on).

It would be easy to suppose that Paul's redefinition of Jewish eschatology around the Messiah and the Spirit functioned on the straightforward principle that he saw the Jewish vision of the end fulfilled already in the Messiah and yet to be fulfilled by the Spirit. But, though there is some truth in this, there are signs that things are (as usual in Paul) more complicated. The still-future judgment on the final day is to be accomplished through the Messiah.[13] On the last day he will perform a key function, namely, the receiving of homage from the whole creation and the handing over of the kingdom to the Father so that – the ultimate in 'God's Future' – God will be all in all.[14] All of this and more is spoken of in the brief but powerful references to the *parousia* of Jesus, to which we shall return. And if the Messiah still has a future role, the Spirit was active in the events which inaugurated this new world, and which are themselves now past events: the Spirit is almost defined, in Romans 8.11, as 'the Spirit of him who raised Jesus from the dead', though it is true that Paul normally speaks of the Messiah's resurrection as being simply by the agency of the Father himself.[15]

But, granted that Paul can make reference to, and use of, the Messiah's future activity and the Spirit's past work, the main thrust of his redefinition of eschatology through the Messiah is of course that what Israel expected God to do for *all* his people at the *end* of time, God has done for the Messiah in the middle of time. This is one of the great centre-points of Paul's thought. It is grounded, of course, in the resurrection of Jesus; it is inconceivable that Paul could have made even the first moves in his eschatological redefinitions had he not believed that Jesus, known to be a messianic pretender of sorts, had been raised from the dead and hence vindicated by God as Messiah and installed as Lord of the world. Of this I have written at length elsewhere.[16]

We can then trace, in Paul's exposition of what God did in Jesus the Messiah, all the key elements of the Jewish eschatology, now reshaped around Jesus. Resurrection: obviously. Messiahship: its immediate consequence.[17] The arrival of God's kingdom: though this theme is nowhere near as central in Paul as it is in the Gospels, his comparatively few references show that he takes it for granted. In particular, though the kingdom is still envisaged as future in 1 Corinthians 6.9, it is present in Romans 14.17 (even though Paul has been talking about the future judgment a few verses earlier), and then, in the fullest passage (1 Corinthians 15.25–29), it is both present and future. In that passage, in a move which may have some antecedents in Jewish thought, he places 'the kingdom of the Messiah' in the present, and the ultimate 'kingdom of God' in the future. 'He must reign until he has put all his enemies under his feet; the last enemy to be destroyed is death; when all things are put in subjection under him, then the Son will himself be subject to the Father, so that God may be all in all.'

Within this theme of God's kingdom, as we already notice in this passage from 1 Corinthians 15, we discover, similarly reimagined, the themes of the great eschatological battle and the defeat of the pagan powers. We have observed before the way in which, in 1 Corinthians 2.7–10 and Colossians 2.14–15, Paul declares that the Messiah has won the contest of strength with the principalities and powers, the rulers both earthly and heavenly. But in 1 Corinthians 15 we see, more fully, the early Christian equivalent of the War Scroll, or of the battle scenes from *Psalms of Solomon* 17 and 18. Like those texts, Paul goes back to the Psalms themselves, not least Psalms 2 and 110: precisely because he believes that Jesus is the Messiah, he discovers that he has already won the victory over the rulers of which those psalms had spoken. The summons of Psalm 2 to the rulers, to be wise because the Messiah has won or will win the victory, looks right across to the Wisdom of Solomon, and Paul must be triangulated with both. The cross of the Messiah serves notice on the powers, and they would not have crucified him had they known that that would happen. His humble obedience to death has resulted in supreme and exalted honour. In particular, he has taken the place reserved in Psalm 8 (echoing Genesis 1 and 2) for the human race: though Paul does not use the phrase 'son of man', and does not draw explicitly on Daniel 2, 7 or 9, his use of Psalm 8 (where the son of man is exalted over the beasts) belongs closely with that whole train of thought in Jewish apocalyptic writing. The dense but explosive summary of the argument in Romans 5.12–21 speaks of Jesus' 'obedience', and the consequent reign of God and his grace, in language which makes most sense within this framework.

As a result, Paul believes that the new Exodus has been launched through the work of Jesus. When he speaks in 1 Corinthians 10 of 'our ancestors' being 'baptized into Moses' and so forth, clearly indicating the parallel with being baptized into the Messiah, he seems to be envisaging Jesus' death as the moment of new Exodus, an impression confirmed, if somewhat kaleidoscopically in terms of theme, by his almost casual reference to the Messiah as the Paschal Lamb (1 Corinthians 5.7). This is then filled out by his large-scale exposition, in Romans 6—8, of the entire Exodus theme as applied to the people of God in Christ. To recapitulate the point: in Romans 6 God's people come through the waters which mean that they are delivered from slavery into freedom; in Romans 7.1—8.11 they come to Sinai only to discover that, though the Torah cannot give the life it promised, God has done it; with the promise of resurrection before them, they are then launched onto the journey of present Christian life, being led by the Spirit through the wilderness and home to the promised land which is the renewal of all creation (8.12–30). This is Paul's version of the retold Exodus story, in loose parallel with the final chapters of the Wisdom of Solomon. It is based, as was Wisdom's retelling, on a fresh reading of the stories of Adam and Abraham (Romans 5 and Romans 4 respectively, out of narrative sequence because of the rhetorical needs of the argument at this point). And this story continues to inform his thinking at many other points.

What then of the return from Exile? How has that been rethought or reimagined? The clearest passage is our old friend Romans 10.5–13, on which I may refer to my commentary for full details. Paul's own exegesis of Deuteronomy 30 indicates, in implicit dialogue with other Jewish readings of this key text, that he believes that in the incarnation, death and resurrection of Jesus the Messiah God fulfilled at last the promise to bring his people back from exile after the long curse. The main difference here with those of his contemporaries who thought like him is that, in parallel with 4 Ezra and some other texts, for Paul the period of Israel's rebellion and (in that sense) 'exile' did not start when the Babylonians captured Jerusalem, but with the time when Torah arrived in Israel – that is, at Mount Sinai.[18] Indeed, even this moment simply made explicit what, for Paul, was already the unrecognized, unnoticed, fact of the case: that all human beings are deemed to be sinners because of Adam. Israel's exile is thus ultimately subsumed under Adam's, and though Paul uses texts which for some of his contemporaries spoke more specifically of a problem which had begun only with Babylon, he appeals with some exegetical justification to the fact that, for instance in Deuteronomy 27—32, Moses himself denounces the people of his day as hard-hearted and bound to break the Law and so incur its curse, culminating in actual geographical exile.

If we take this as a basic reference point, there are several other passages which come out in a new light, not least the much-contested Galatians 3.10–14. The point about the 'curse', and the Messiah's bearing it on behalf of others, is not that there is a general, abstract curse hanging over the whole human race. Paul's argument never quite makes sense if we try to get at it like that. The whole chapter is far more specifically about the place of ethnic Israel within God's long-term purpose to give Abraham a single worldwide family.

This is how the passage works.[19] God made promises to Abraham, promises about a family from all nations, who would be justified, declared to be in the right, on the basis of faith rather than Torah. In fact, Paul insists, all who are 'in' or 'under' Torah – in other words, as we see throughout his writings, the Jewish people – are under the curse. He has Deuteronomy specifically in mind, and there the curse is of course 'exile', whether we take it here literally or metaphorically. As in Romans 2.17–24, the problem with claiming Torah is that both Torah and Prophets declare that Israel is cursed and exiled because of breaking Torah. That, at least, is the most immediate problem. The larger and longer-term problem, a problem for God in terms of his having made promises to Abraham about the future worldwide family, is that the pagan nations do not receive the blessing of Abraham, which God had promised him to give them. Worse, as Paul says in Romans 2.24, they are actually blaspheming Abraham's God because of Abraham's family. The curse which has come upon Israel has thus caused the promises made *through* Israel to get stuck; and it is this curse, with this result, from which, according to Galatians 3.10–14, the Messiah has redeemed 'us'.

This can be seen clearly from the punchline at the end of the paragraph, always a good indication of where the writer at least supposes the train of thought is going. The Messiah's 'becoming a curse for us' by being hanged on a tree means two very specific things (not the generalized atonement so often envisaged at this point): first, that the blessing of Abraham might after all come upon the Gentiles; second, that 'we' – by which Paul must mean specifically Jewish Christians – might receive the promise of the Spirit through faith. (Of course, Gentiles also receive the promise of the Spirit through faith, but Paul is making a particular point here, that whereas Gentiles are reached by the promises for the first time, ethnic Jews who believe the gospel have their membership in God's people renewed.)

Galatians 3 is a fascinating argument in itself; but I go into it here to show that Paul's exegesis of Deuteronomy 30 in Romans 10 is not a flash in the pan. It represents a well-established train of thought on which he could draw in various ways at different times. He believes that, in the work of Jesus, God has brought the curse of exile to an end, has moved the great narrative on to its new point, and has opened up the new phase of history. By rethinking all this Jewish eschatology around the Messiah, and by locating this work in the past, Paul has firmly anchored his inaugurated eschatology in the story of Israel that has reached its *telos* in Jesus, particularly in his death and resurrection.

Resurrection; Messiah; kingdom of God; new exodus; end of exile; so far, so good. Paul is clearly working with, and reimagining around Jesus, the traditional themes of Jewish eschatology, and showing that in each case that which was expected at the end has at least begun to happen within the ongoing course of history. What then of the still-future eschatology focused on the Messiah? Here I return to some passages I treated briefly from another angle earlier in this book. It has sometimes been said, astonishingly enough but supposedly on the basis of my work on Jesus, that I have systematically denied the doctrine of the 'second coming'. Nothing could be further from the truth, though of course this, too, needs cleaning up in the light of what the New Testament actually says as opposed to what sundry would-be Christian traditions have made of it. For some, alas, the very phrase 'second coming', and even perhaps the word 'eschatology' itself, conjures up visions of the 'rapture' as understood within some branches of (mostly North American) fundamentalist or evangelical Christianity, and as set out, at a popular level, in the 'Left Behind' series of novels by Tim F. Lahaye and Jerry B. Jenkins, and the theology, if you can call it that, which those books embody.[20] That scheme of thought, ironically considering its fanatical though bizarre support for the present state of Israel, is actually deeply un-Jewish, collapsing into a dualism in which the present wicked world is left to stew in its own juice while the saints are snatched up to heaven to watch Armageddon from a ringside seat.

This is massively different from anything we find in Paul, for all that the central text for the 'rapture' theology is of course 1 Thessalonians 4.16–17. What we find in Paul at this point is four things, in each of which we see the still-future Jewish eschatology redrawn around the Messiah.[21] First, there is the 'Day of the Lord' or 'Day of the Messiah', a redefinition of the older 'Day of YHWH'. Second, there is his *parousia*, his royal presence or appearing, with the imperial connotations as well as divine ones sometimes brought out by the word *epiphaneia*. Third, there is his *judgment*, his bringing at last of God's wise justice and order to the whole creation. Fourth, there is as a result the renewal of all creation as it pays homage to him. A few words about each are in order, not least to point out that these, too, though still future from Paul's perspective, are not in fact as utterly final as we sometimes think.

A case in point is the first, the 'Day of the Lord'. It is uncontroversial to point out that this is Paul's reworking of the Jewish 'Day of YHWH' traditions; but it is highly controversial to point out, as I did in the Chapter 3, that for Paul 'the Day of the Lord' by no means denoted the end of the world. Just as in Amos or Jeremiah the really appalling thing about the 'Day of YHWH' was that there would be another day after it – had it been the actual end of the world it would have been a shame, but there wouldn't have been anybody around to worry about it after it had happened – so in Paul the 'Day of the

Lord' is clearly something which might well happen during the continuing lifetimes of himself and his readers. It is something you might hear about by letter. Nevertheless, it is a great moment of judgment as a result of which everything will be different, and the world will be changed. Normally as a historian I eschew the temptation to address the question of 'What might have happened if . . .', 'What people would have said if . . .', and so on. But I have no hesitation in saying that, had Paul been alive in the year we call AD 70, when the convulsions in Rome during the Year of the Four Emperors were quickly followed by the destruction of Jerusalem, he would have said, 'That's it. That's the Day of the Lord.' I think, in fact, that this is precisely what the notorious passage in 1 Thessalonians 2.16 is referring to: God's wrath has come upon them *eis telos*, in a climactic and decisive way. That is the most immediate thing from which Paul wants to see his contemporaries rescued. Of course, as in Jeremiah, there may then be other 'Days of the Lord'. But that is the one which writes into history, within a generation of Jesus' death and resurrection, the fact that the powers which opposed him and put him on the cross – that is, the Roman empire with the connivance of the Jewish hierarchy – were incurring their own judgment.

Second, there is the *parousia*, about which I spoke in Chapters 3 and 4. To recapitulate briefly: the word *parousia* itself is not an Old Testament word, but seems to be borrowed from the language of the court, of princes and emperors. It is what happens when a king is making a state visit to a city, or indeed returning to Rome after a journey or battle. He appears, and is thus 'present', as opposed to 'absent', in his royal pomp. This is, indeed, one of the ways in which, in this redrawn eschatology, Paul keeps the anti-pagan emphasis fully in play: what counts is the *parousia* not of Caesar, but of Jesus. But Paul is still working within the controlling Jewish stories now retold around Jesus; and his high Christology enables him at this point to pull in also the theme of the return of YHWH to Zion, which as I have suggested was one of the main (mostly secret, though eventually revealed) themes of Jesus' own awareness of vocation, and which dominated some strands of Jewish eschatology in the period. Thus the pagan theme of the 'royal presence' of Caesar is upstaged, and the Jewish theme of the coming of YHWH simultaneously fulfilled, in Paul's rich theology of the *parousia* of Jesus.[22] Once again 1 Thessalonians 4 and 1 Corinthians 15 are central.

We should note again, in addition, the ways in which Paul can also speak of Jesus' 'appearing', rather than his 'arrival' as though from a great distance. Paul's Jewish cosmology of heaven and earth had, no doubt, been itself redrawn around the Messiah and Spirit. But part of that redrawing was that the close and intimate presence of the one who, for a Jewish worshipper, dwells in heaven was embodied for Paul in the close and intimate presence of the Jesus who, now in heaven, was constantly interceding to the Father on our behalf.[23] And when the one who was now in heaven finally appeared, revealing his royal presence, this was not to be thought of in terms of his making a long journey from a far country. It would be more like drawing back a previously unnoticed curtain to reveal what had been there all along. Granted, that revelation would be literally earth-shattering, but that is simply the necessary and inevitable effect of the final coming together of heaven and earth, not anything to do with a 'coming' as often envisaged in popular presentations. Our citizenship, Paul says, is in heaven, and from there we await the Saviour, the Lord, Jesus the King – which means, despite many misreadings, not that we will in the end go off to heaven, but that the one who is presently in heaven will come back and transform the earth, where we have lived as a colonial outpost of heaven waiting for that day.[24] We noted in Chapter 4 that these are basically Caesar-titles, deliberately employed at this point. We now return to the passage to emphasize that Paul does *not* say that at Jesus' *parousia* his people will be taken up into heaven to live with him there. That is the dualistic perversion of a genuine New Testament second-coming theology. The point of Jesus coming 'from' heaven is that he will change both this old world and our present bodies. The idea of 'changing' is of course closely cognate here with what, in 1 Corinthians 15.50–54, Paul says will happen to those left alive at the *parousia*.

Day of YHWH; *parousia*; and third, judgment. This is of course a major theme in the Old Testament and subsequent Jewish literature. Despite those who have wanted to insist that 'works' never come into Paul's mind in a positive sense, he clearly envisages not only a future judgment at the *bēma tou Christou*, the Messiah's judgment-seat, but also that this judgment will be in accordance with the entirety of the life that has been led. But this is not our present theme. For the moment we simply note that Paul has effortlessly and naturally given to Jesus the role marked out in so much Jewish thought for the Messiah. This is not, by now, unexpected, but it is another clear signpost of how his thinking works. Once more, he is not only drawing on Jewish themes – and, at this point, controverting any suggestion that there might be a 'favoured nation clause' for the Jewish people, by insisting that all alike must stand before the Messiah and his judgment – but also standing over against the natural pagan assumptions. Within paganism, there was little if any idea of a post-mortem judgment, though there were some schemes of thought which had tried to propose something like one. But there was plenty of judgment in the present, by the self-styled World's True Lord and his henchmen. The coming just judgment of the Messiah was both the fulfilment of the age-old Jewish hope, the answer to so many prayers in the Psalms and elsewhere, and also the final statement, like that of Daniel to Nebuchadnezzar, that the Lord Most High rules over the kingdoms of mortals. The fact that Paul can so easily indicate that the people of the Messiah will themselves sit in judgment, even over angels,[25] indicates how fully he has rethought the Jewish picture of coming judgment, based on Daniel 7 as well as elsewhere, around Jesus both as the embodiment of YHWH and as the inclusive representative of God's people.

Fourth, and consequent upon this, there is the great theme of the renewal of all creation through the Messiah. I have already referred to Colossians 1.15–20 in some detail, and simply need to note here that when Paul declares, there and in Ephesians 1, that it is now God's intention both to reconcile all things to, through and for him and to sum up all things in the Messiah, he is standing firmly against all kinds of dualism which would envisage a final state in which the present created order was abandoned as worthless. Just as at the end of Revelation the new heavens and the new earth are joined together, so in Paul's thought the triumphant goal of eschatology is that there should be one future for the one world made and loved by the one God. For God to be all in all, as in 1 Corinthians 15.28, it is necessary that, through the Messiah's victory over death itself, the ultimate corruption of the present world and its inhabitants, creation can be set free from its bondage to decay and share the freedom of the glory of God's children. Thus the picture is complete: Paul has reimagined every single aspect of first-century Jewish eschatology around Jesus the Messiah and his death and resurrection.

This is seen to good effect in Romans 8; but, since that passage is more particularly about the Spirit, it will serve as a convenient bridge to cross into the second half of this chapter. As with everything else, Paul had reimagined – reworked – re*lived* his traditional Jewish eschatology around not only the Messiah but also the Spirit.

4. Eschatology Reimagined around the Spirit

In order to prepare for our reading of Romans 8, we begin further away, with Paul's eschatological sense of the fresh outpouring of the Spirit. I noted in the previous chapter that the reference to Joel in Romans 10.13 was to be taken as an oblique reference to the Spirit and the renewal of the covenant: in a confluence of texts including Ezekiel 36 and Jeremiah 31, Paul saw the covenant renewal, effected by the Spirit, as the inauguration in the present of that eschatological state in which (a) Gentiles were brought from outside to inside and (b) Jews were renewed from within, as both together were grasped by the gospel and, through baptism, were brought into the eschatological people of God, the Messiah's Body. This corresponds to what we saw already in Galatians 3.14, and more especially 4.6–7: 'Because you, Jew and Gentile alike, are God's children, God has sent the Spirit of his son into our hearts, crying Abba, father.'

The outpouring of the Spirit was confused in Corinth, as indeed it has been in twentieth-century Christian speech, with the variety of religious phenomena on offer in the ancient world as in the modern. Only in late secularism could it be supposed that phenomena like speaking in tongues were automatically a sign that the one true God was at work; Paul, who knew plenty about other supernatural phenomena outside Christianity, was going to take more convincing. The theology of the Spirit which he hammers out in 1 Corinthians, a central part of his polemic against the wisdom of the present age, is all to do with the fact that the new age has broken in and that the Spirit will enable ex-pagan Christians to live in accordance with it. This, as I said before, is characteristic of his inaugurated eschatology all through. The final statement of God's future in chapter 15 is not a detached statement of the Last Things, stuck on the end of a letter which is otherwise about other topics. It is a summary of what the letter has been about all the way through. If the Corinthians will only grasp the way in which God's new age had broken in to the world through the death and resurrection of Jesus, and the fact that they have been summoned to live in that new age rather than in the present evil age, most of the issues addressed in the letter will fall into line.[26]

In the same way, the problems Paul addresses in 2 Corinthians will likewise become clear. Faced with a head-on challenge to his authority, Paul's mode of response is precisely to expound the theology of the new covenant, in which (as we saw in the previous chapter) the community has been redefined. It is because he and they are both living, by the Spirit, in God's new age that they are enabled to see in one another's unveiled faces the glory of God. This treasure is hidden in earthen vessels, whose suffering masks – to the viewpoint of the present world, in which outward success is what matters – the appearance of the true glory. But the point of the eschatological suffering, here as in Romans 5.1–5, is that now the apostle is not only enabled to bear suffering without illusion and without despair but is also enabled to see, in it, the bodying forth of the dying and rising of the Messiah. The hidden work of the Spirit enables the apostle to re-embody the Messiah as the herald of his new age, against the day when the Spirit will make all things new.

This brings us to one of the major eschatological tasks Paul ascribes to the Spirit: that of being the *arrabōn*, the down payment, of what is to come. The Spirit is a gift from God's future, the gift which guarantees that future. This theme is grounded in 2 Corinthians in particular,[27] but it is introduced as well almost casually in Romans and Ephesians.[28] The new covenant work of the Spirit, transforming the heart so as to enable it to keep the commandments of the Torah, is the sign that God's new age has broken in in respect of this person too.[29] This is made known, it seems, first and foremost in the prayed expression of experienced sonship – what we might loosely call Paul's understanding of Christian spirituality – but also in what we have often, and misleadingly, called 'ethics'. This brings us to Galatians 5, where the point of the passage about the Spirit and the flesh is by no means to be reduced to a set of rules for Christian observance. Paul constantly gives us signs that that is the wrong way to read what he is saying. His main point, rather, is that if you are walking by the Spirit you are clearly already part of God's new age and his renewed people, part of that inaugurated-eschatological family who have been delivered from the present evil age – and, as such, you are 'not under the Torah'.[30] The Torah has nothing more to say about you. As he says later, having just described all kinds of character traits which the Spirit produces, there is no Torah against such behaviour.[31]

Now at last, with the full vision of Paul's rethinking of his Jewish tradition opening up before us, we are able to see more fully why it was that Paul held and developed his critique of Israel – the point at which so much debate about the so-called 'new perspective' has simply got stuck. The point was neither simply that Paul saw Judaism as a religion of legalism and Christianity as a religion of grace (the old perspective); nor simply that Paul found salvation in Christ and therefore deduced that it wasn't available in Judaism after all (Sanders's own version of the new perspective). It was, first and foremost, a matter of *eschatology*: God had acted in Jesus the Messiah to usher in the new age, to inaugurate the new covenant, to plant the seeds of new creation. The preaching of the gospel was the means whereby the Spirit worked in the hearts and minds of both Jews and Gentiles not just to give them a new religious experience, not even just to bring them salvation, but to make them the people in whom the new age, the Age to Come of Jewish eschatological expectation, had come to birth. The work of the gospel, by the Spirit, in the individual Christian is the putting-to-rights in advance of men, women and children, against the day when God puts the whole world to rights; what is more, that initial putting-to-rights by the power of the gospel is simultaneously, and necessarily, a vocation to each person thus 'justified' to enlist in the ongoing work, by the Spirit, of making God's saving, restorative justice as much of a reality as possible in the present age, in advance of the final putting-to-rights of the whole creation. This is the point at which 'justification by faith' can be firmly located on the map of Paul's reimagining of Jewish eschatology in the light of Jesus and the Spirit.

That is why Christian ethics is so much more than keeping a new law. It is living in the new age. In particular, that is why, in 1 Corinthians 13, Paul expounds the life of love not so much as a new duty but as the Christian's new *destiny*: faith, hope and supremely love are the things that will last, the qualities which, as fruits of the Spirit, are the bridges into the new world, and by learning to cross those bridges we are already living by the rule, as Paul can still sometimes call it, of God's new creation. This is why, too, though Paul does not always mention the Spirit when he says such things, he can claim that the one who began a good work in you will bring it to completion at the day of the Messiah.[32]

And that is why, in particular, the Spirit is the path by which Paul traces the route from justification by faith in the present to justification, by the complete life lived, in the future. You cannot understand justification by faith in Romans 3 and 4 unless you see it flanked by the long statement of judgment according to works in Romans 2.1–16 and the spectacular scene in Romans 8 which explains why there is indeed 'no condemnation for those who are in the Messiah, Jesus'. This is the point at which the redefinition of justification which I offered in the previous chapter makes its presence fully felt: because if by 'justification' you suppose that Paul means 'the event by which you become a Christian', this is always going to sound contested, as though (to quote one of my critics) one were smuggling in a semi-Pelagianism by the back door, insisting, in the teeth of Galatians 3, that having begun with faith one must end with works after all. It simply isn't like that – and Galatians 3, being about circumcision, makes the point, because Paul did not see circumcision at all as a 'good work' which one might do as part of a self-help moralism, but always as an ethnic badge. Rather, the point about faith is that it is the first-fruit of the work of the Spirit, operating in the human heart through the preaching of the gospel. No one can say, 'Jesus is Lord', except by the Spirit; 'by grace you are saved through faith, and that not of yourselves, it is God's gift'.[33] The point then, laid out in Romans 8.1–11, is this: the verdict already issued over Christian faith in Romans 3 does indeed genuinely anticipate the verdict to be issued over the entirety of the life led, because the Spirit now at work in you, the Spirit because of whose presence you are beginning to walk according to the Spirit and not according to the flesh, is the Spirit of the God who raised Jesus from the dead, and hence the Spirit through whom God will raise all those who belong to the Messiah.[34] This is why, when Paul looks ahead to the future and asks, as well one might, what God will say on the last day, he holds up as his joy and crown, not the merits and death of Jesus, but the churches he has planted who remain faithful to the gospel.[35] The path from initial faith to final resurrection (and resurrection, we must remind ourselves, constitutes rescue, that is, salvation, from death itself) lies through holy and faithful Spirit-led service, including suffering.

This then – to glance ahead to the end of Romans 8 – is part of the reason why Paul celebrates the assurance of final salvation: if God is for us, who is against us? The Spirit is not mentioned in Romans 8.31–39, but that is because Paul is in fact *doing* that which one does when the Spirit is at work, rather than, on this occasion, talking about it: this celebration, this exultation in God's saving power, is what he means when he speaks of love for God being poured out in our hearts through the Holy Spirit.[36]

But the Spirit is of course one of the major themes in 8.12–30, to which at last we return. This is the place par excellence where the Spirit has redefined Jewish eschatology. As we noted, the passage is rooted in Paul's telling of the new-exodus story, and in that story the Spirit takes the place of the Shekinah, the tabernacling presence of YHWH with his people as they journey through the wilderness to the promised land. This is the real return from exile, the exile in which Adam and Eve found themselves expelled from a free, deathless Eden.[37] The end of exile, the undoing of creation's bondage to decay, will come about (according to Jeremiah and Ezekiel) through the new covenant; very well, declares Paul, that is what has happened in Christ and by the Spirit.

The Spirit is then the one who conforms the Messiah's people to his suffering and glory, so that the Jewish expectation of the coming Messiah is fulfilled not just in the Messiah himself, but, extraordinarily, in his people as well.[38] The Spirit is the one who enables God's people to endure suffering without illusion but also without despair. We may even be right to suggest that, through the Spirit, the Christian engages in the present with the ongoing battle which derives from the victory on the cross. To put it another way, the ethical struggles of the Christian are the beginning of that sovereign rule over the created order which will be fulfilled in the new world. One's own body is, so to speak, the small part of the created world over which one is given advance responsibility, against the day when much will be given to those from whom much, in the present, has been expected. When God's children are finally revealed in their new, glorious bodies, then the whole creation will have its own exodus, its own liberation. We can only guess at what that will actually look like. But we can be sure that it, too, will be accomplished by the same Spirit of the living God. And, since the Spirit is given to us in the present as a down payment, we are charged already with implementing that ultimate accomplishment. We are called to produce, in a thousand different ways, signs of God's new world within the apparently unpromising landscape of the old one.

This happens, at its core, through the presence of the Spirit in the groaning of prayer. The two little verses on prayer are not intended at this point as simply an aside to encourage devotion.[39] They are the very heart of Paul's reworked, and inaugurated, eschatology. The reason we do not know what to pray for as we ought is that we are caught in the overlap of the ages, and can only see through a glass, darkly; but God the Spirit intercedes for us with groanings too deep for words. Our word 'ethics', and for that matter our words 'prayer' and 'spirituality', are not, it seems, labels which we can stick accurately on certain things we do and then take for granted. They are long-range signposts to a reality which lies deeper in God's dark purposes than we normally imagine. And in the middle of that darkness there lies the secret of God's new world, the secret which will burst out at last when the earth shall be filled with the glory of God as the waters cover the sea. That is the point at which God will be all in all, at which God will truly be God, at which the future which God intends for the world and the future which God intends for himself come together into one glorious reality.

5. Eschatology in Context

Before we conclude this chapter, a word about each of the other angles of vision which, as in the previous two chapters, slice through Paul's reworking of the central Jewish doctrines. First, in all that he does he is engaged in implicit dialogue both with the Old Testament itself and with other first-century readings of it. His vision of the end of all things is derived from the Old Testament, ultimately from the story of creation itself; note the way in which Genesis 1—3 lies near the heart both of Romans 8 and of 1 Corinthians 15. His focus on Jesus and the Spirit means that at point after point he is saying, *this* is how the scriptures have been fulfilled, as opposed to other ways in which other Jews might suppose they would be fulfilled; his vision of God's final battle against cosmic evil presents both a parallel and a stark contrast to the vision so dramatically expressed in the War Scroll. Jesus, not some other figure, is the long-awaited

Messiah; his resurrection is the first stage in a two-stage resurrection which has radically redefined that central Jewish doctrine; the Spirit whom Paul knows as 'the Spirit of the God who raised Jesus', not some other spirit, is the one through whose work the covenant is renewed; conversely, the covenant has been renewed in Jesus the Messiah and through the Spirit, not through some other means (say, the work of the Teacher of Righteousness, or some new kind of Torah-piety). In these and many other ways it would be possible to show that Paul's reimagining of Jewish eschatology is grounded in a fresh, and often controversial or even polemical, reading of scripture.

Second, Paul's reimagined eschatology retains the central Jewish emphasis of confrontation with paganism. Paul continued to believe that when God finally acted in fulfilment of his promises he would call the whole world to account, and in particular that he would judge and condemn that idolatry and wickedness which the Jewish people saw as characteristic of the pagan world, and which some Jews at least, notably the great prophets, saw as tragically characteristic of Israel also. Paul's reimagining of Jewish eschatology led him to speak of Jesus himself as the coming judge, to highlight the fact that Jews and Gentiles were indeed on a level before that judgment, and to see the work of the Spirit as calling out a people who would escape the condemnation.[40] As a result, we are not surprised to find that the political confrontation characteristic of so much Jewish eschatology continues in Paul in christological mode: some of Paul's classic statements about Jesus involve his installation and enthronement as the universal sovereign of the world, with the whole world bowing the knee at his name.[41] It is his 'arrival' and 'glorious appearing', not that of Caesar, that will bring true order and justice to the world.[42] Within this setting of a reimagined ultimate eschatology we can sense, too, the force of Paul's inaugurated-eschatological ethic, seen to good advantage in a passage like 1 Corinthians 6 and given theological grounding in Romans 6. The point is not, 'Here are a few new rules for you to live by', but rather, 'Because you already live in the new age, you must no longer behave in the way that the pagan world behaves'.[43] It is Jesus' victory over death, on the one hand, and the Spirit's work within, on the other, that will make real this eschatological victory over pagan behaviour.[44]

Paul achieves all this without ever collapsing into dualism. It is possible to avoid the corruptions of the world by avoiding the world itself, but he never makes that mistake. For Paul, creation is good, and is to be redeemed; indeed, it has already been redeemed in the resurrection of Jesus the Messiah. This victory will one day be complete, and that final goal must be anticipated in the celebratory ethical living of God's people in the present. Paganism worships some parts of the created order and, paradoxically, connives thereby at the decay and corruption of creation itself. Judaism worships the creator, celebrates the goodness of creation, and looks for its rescue from decay. Paul declares that this rescue has already been accomplished through the Messiah, that it is being accomplished by the Spirit who puts the Messiah's work into operation in the present, and that it will be accomplished in the fresh act whereby God will be all in all.

Third, Paul's reimagined eschatology was put to work in his day-to-day tasks of announcing the gospel and bringing God's wise ordering to the churches which came into being as a result of his preaching. His sense of the apostolic task, so alien to the Corinthians and their expectations, grew directly out of his sense of where his work was to be located within the eschatological plan of God: God has put us apostles on show right at the end, he writes, like men condemned to death.[45] He exercised authority over the churches with that strange mixture of weakness and power, rooted in the death and resurrection of Jesus and energized by the Spirit, of which he writes so movingly in 2 Corinthians. When he acts in discipline, it is to anticipate the final judgment, to bring it forward into the present so that the church may in this way, too, be the eschatological people of God.[46] Paul acted, and understood himself to be acting, as the herald of the cosmic good news which had now at last been declared to the whole world.[47] This is a vital element in our understanding of his actual practice. As he wrote to the Thessalonians, his view of what he was doing, and of what he and his converts were suffering, was set in the context of his belief that God was calling them all alike into his kingdom and glory.[48] Only when Paul's apostolic practice is seen in the light of his reimagined eschatology will his work, and the life of his communities, be understood in its proper dimensions. This is not to marginalize sociological study of Paul and his churches, but to set such study within its appropriate context.

6. Conclusion

My theological proposal is now complete. I have laid out at least in outline the Jewish doctrines of monotheism, election and eschatology as Paul would have known them, and I have argued that we can best understand his theology in terms of his redefinition, his rethinking, of these doctrines around the twin poles of Messiah and Spirit. This has led him at point after point to retell the great stories which his fellow Jews told, both as now fulfilled through Jesus the Messiah and as looking for their final fulfilment at the day of Christ, when at the coming judgment the Spirit would do for all Jesus' people what God had done for Jesus himself, that is, would raise them from the dead. God's victory over evil, more particularly paganism both religious and political, the new exodus and the end of exile, the coming kingdom of God and the rule of the Messiah, even the return of YHWH to Zion – all are reworked through Paul's gospel. This cannot, I suggest, be an accident. I have not attempted to compare this outline proposal with the other ones regularly on offer in Pauline studies, since I have preferred fresh exposition of primary sources to sidelong engagement with secondary ones. But I hope it at least provides a fruitful seedbed for future research and fresh insight.

The thesis I have advanced to this point raises three questions. First, what is the relation of the Paul I have described to Jesus himself? Second, how did Paul's actual practice, his life and work as an apostle, embody and reflect the theology he expounded? Third, how does the Pauline theology I have outlined relate to the tasks of the church at the start of the twenty-first century? Each of these topics would happily take an entire further book. But in order to point the way towards further work, not simply for myself but for any who might like to undertake it, I shall attempt to summarize, in the final chapter, these three among many lines of enquiry which now lie open before us.

8

Jesus, Paul and the Task of the Church

1. Introduction

I want in this concluding chapter to attempt a threefold task by way both of summing up where the argument has brought us and pointing to some questions and corollaries. The centrepiece is the question of how all this theology worked out in practice in Paul's actual apostolic labour. In conclusion, I want to venture some musings on our reappropriation of the Paul I have been describing within our postmodern context. But I want to turn first to a brief discussion of the question which has vexed New Testament scholars, and many in the church and the wider world, for many years: the question of Jesus and Paul. Until we address this we are not in fact ready to grasp why Paul's own ministry was what it was.

2. Jesus and Paul

The question of the relation between Jesus and Paul has normally been posed in the wrong terms. I am going to suggest that once we put it in the right framework the perceived problem disappears and re-emerges as a powerful indicator of the true nature of early Christianity.[1]

The problem has been posed in terms of the apparent mismatch between the teaching of Jesus and Paul. One normal way of stating it goes like this: Jesus preached about God but Paul preached about Jesus. Or, if you like, Jesus announced the kingdom of God, Paul announced the Messiahship of Jesus. This plays out in other ways: Jesus called people to a simple gospel of repentance, belief and the practice of the Sermon on the Mount; Paul developed a complex theology of justification by faith, something Jesus never mentioned, with all kinds of hard and gritty bits quite alien to the original message. At this point, of course, there are two parallel tracks on which the critique begins to diverge. Some say that Jesus preached a wonderful universal message and that Paul scrunched it back into the small and distorting framework of his Jewish, especially rabbinic, mind. Others say that Jesus preached a pure Jewish message and that Paul falsified it by turning it into a Greek, philosophical and even anti-Jewish construct.

These various ways of polarizing Jesus and Paul, and other variations, simply miss the point. They assume that Jesus and Paul were both trying, essentially, to do the same kind of thing, namely, to preach and teach a set of theological, religious and/or ethical truths, and that one can therefore line up the various elements of what we know of their sayings and play them off against one another. But my whole line of thought throughout this book insists that this is simply the wrong way of going about it. The framework in which we have to look at Jesus and Paul is not at all that of abstract teaching and preaching, so that one might compare them as one does with Plato and Aristotle, or even Luther and Calvin. Both of them lived and thought within the kind of thematic synthesis which I laid out in Chapters 2, 3 and 4, namely that of creation and covenant, Messiahship and apocalyptic, gospel and empire. And when we ask where they belong within that set of themes we see that it would have been very surprising if Paul *had* said the same kinds of things as Jesus. Indeed, had he done so he would have falsified the message of Jesus, not underscored it.

How so? The relationship between them, as Paul himself conceived it, was not at all like that of a second-generation rabbi determined to pass on as much as possible of what the original master had said. Nor was it like that of a second-generation reformer – to think again of Luther and Calvin – developing the original insights with certain significant modifications. The relationship between them, as far as Paul was concerned, was much more like that between a composer and a conductor; or between a medical researcher and a doctor; or between an architect and a builder. The composer writes the music; if the conductor decided to write some on his own account, that would be a way of saying he didn't want to play that composer's music, but some of his own instead. His job is to *play* the music the original composer has written. The doctor takes the results of the research and applies them to the patient. Her job is not to do more research on the topic; or, if she thinks it is, it isn't because she is being loyal to the original researcher but because she is being disloyal. The builder takes the plans drawn up by the architect and builds to that design. It isn't his task to draw a new building; or, if he does, it's not because he is filled with admiration for the original design but because he isn't.

I apologize for labouring the point; but in my experience of teaching, and also in public debate, not least media debate, about Jesus and Paul, I have been made aware again and again that within our post-Enlightenment world the pressure to resist the covenantal and apocalyptic framework for both Jesus and Paul – the pressure, more or less, to de-Judaize both of them, or to allow only one of them to be 'Jewish' and then only within a post-Enlightenment version of what 'Judaism' might be – this pressure has been intense, and conversely the pressure to treat them both as abstract religious teachers, or as parallel preachers of a doctrine of salvation, has been as enormous as it is insidious. It is the default mode into which our culture slips when faced with the whole topic. It isn't the case that there is a range of options out there in contemporary public discourse. Rather, the minute we stop applying the pressure for a genuine first-century framework of covenant, apocalyptic and so on people's minds automatically flip back into this abstract mode. 'But surely,' they say, even after a careful explanation to the contrary, 'but surely Paul had some very different ideas from Jesus?' – with the constant implication that this relativizes Paul, that this means we can appeal over Paul's head to Jesus himself, which usually means a Jesus reconstructed according to one of the post-Enlightenment Procrustean beds currently available from all good bookshops.

I have argued elsewhere that Jesus believed himself to be bringing to its great climax, its great denouement, the long story of YHWH and Israel, which was the focal point of the long story of the creator and the world. I have proposed that he believed himself to be embodying *both* the vocation of faithful Israel *and* the return of YHWH to Zion, drawing on to himself not only the destiny of God's true Servant but, if we can put it like this, the destiny of God himself. All this would be a very odd, not to say an embarrassingly weird, thing for a post-Enlightenment person to believe about Jesus – though we ought to point out that the great thinkers who invented the concept of the Enlightenment in the first place really do seem to have thought that world history was turning a new corner with their own work, leaving behind superstition and ignorance and stepping at last into the bright light of scientific, technological, political and philosophical modernity. The Enlightenment, in fact, offered an *alternative eschatology* to that of Jesus and Paul: world history didn't after all reach its climax with the death and resurrection of the Messiah, but with Voltaire, Rousseau and Thomas Jefferson. The guillotine, not the cross, provided the redemptive violence around which the world turned. No wonder thinkers within this framework of thought found it hard to see Jesus within his genuinely first-century Jewish world, and to understand the way in which Paul was explicitly honouring Jesus by *not* saying and doing the same things but by pointing people back to Jesus' own unique achievement.

How does this work out in terms of the respective roles which Jesus and Paul each believed themselves to be playing? It isn't even that Jesus believed himself to have a specific role in the purpose of God and that Paul simply thought that people like himself ought to tell people about Jesus. Paul, too, believed himself to have a special, unique role within the overall purposes of Israel's God, the world's creator; and that role was precisely not to bring Israel's history to its climax – that had been done in the death and resurrection of the Messiah – but rather to perform the next unique task within an implicit apocalyptic timetable, namely to call the nations, urgently, to loyal submission to the one who had now been enthroned as Lord of the world. Paul believed that it was his task to call into being, by proclaiming Jesus as Lord, the worldwide community in which ethnic divisions would be abolished and a new family created as a sign to the watching world that Jesus was its rightful Lord and that new creation had been launched and would one day come to full flower. That points us forward to the specific apostolic tasks which Paul set himself, to which I shall turn in a moment. But let me apply this briefly to three major areas where the normal paradigm has raised problems: the kingdom of God, justification and ethics.

First, the kingdom of God. Why does Jesus say so much about it and Paul so little?

Part of the answer must be that Jesus was addressing a Jewish world in which 'kingdom of God', 'reign of God', the notion that only God must be king, was one of the most exciting and dangerous slogans. People had died in recent memory because of this slogan and the attempt to put it into practice. Galilee and Judaea were full of young men who were eager to take upon themselves the yoke of the kingdom, that is, to work for the holy revolution against the western imperial power, whatever it cost. (The overtones of our contemporary world are not accidental.) They were drawing on the centuries-old tradition of psalms and prophets, living within the narrative world generated, as the earlier chapters of this book have indicated, out of that matrix of creation and covenant, apocalyptic and messianism, the world in which Israel stood proud, at least in theory, against paganism, its idolatries and its empires. Jesus was living within that world, too, but was offering a radically different construal of what it should mean, what the true God wanted it to mean, and what, focused upon himself and his work, it was now beginning to mean. Much of his kingdom-teaching was located within his work of healing and feasting, of *doing* the kingdom in fresh ways; and his many kingdom-parables were ways of saying, *this*, not something else, is what God's kingdom is all about. Within the political and cultural climate of the time, to say that one was embracing the kingdom-vision but doing it significantly differently was hugely risky. Parables and symbolic actions were the natural best ways of doing it.

Paul knew all about that world, but it was not the world in which he was called to work. This does *not* mean that he swapped a Jewish message for a Gentile or Hellenistic one. Rather, he announced a still very Jewish message, namely, the message that Israel's crucified and risen Messiah was the true Lord of the world, to a world which was not telling, and living by, Jewish-style kingdom-of-God stories. There would have been no point in Paul standing up in the market place in Philippi and saying, 'I'll tell you what the kingdom of God is really like.' That wasn't what people in Philippi were talking about, or eager for. But standing up and saying, 'Let me tell you the true gospel of the real Lord of the world' – that would have all kinds of resonances which I explored in Chapter 4. For Paul, then, 'kingdom of God' had become part of the package of how to explain what Jesus had already accomplished through his death and resurrection, the accomplishment which now had to be implemented.

What then about 'justification by faith'? Why is this so important for Paul but not, it seems, for Jesus? There is of course a lone passage in Luke's gospel, the parable of the Pharisee and the tax-collector, where Jesus says that 'this man went down to his house justified rather than the other'.[2] But this is hardly, as it stands, a statement either of the mainstream Protestant doctrine of justification or of the rather different Pauline one. It is a straightforward Jewish statement, corresponding for instance to Judah's statement about Tamar, after his immorality and hypocrisy have been exposed ('she is in the right, rather than me'): one is in the right, the other is in the wrong.[3] There is an implicit court case going on, and the verdict is going in favour of one person rather than the other.

The implicit court case is of course important in Paul's world of thought, as I have suggested, but once again we meet the question of *context and task*. The doctrine of justification by faith, from Galatians through Philippians to Romans, was never about how people were to be converted, how someone might become a Christian, but about how one could *tell*, in the present, who God's true people were – and hence who one's family were, who were the people with whom one should, as a matter of family love and loyalty, sit down and eat. This question was central to much Judaism of the time, with different groups defining themselves this way and that, in particular by various interpretations of Torah. We can already see the roots of this redefinition of God's people in Jesus' ministry, not simply when the language of justification is fleetingly used as in Luke 18, but at many other moments like Mark 3.31–35 (the redefinition of family) and Luke 15.1–2 (why does Jesus eat with tax-collectors and sinners?). But Jesus never faced, for the reasons already given, the question of how one would know that *Gentiles* were to be full members of God's people. The closest he comes is at moments like Matthew 8.11 ('many will come from east and west and sit down with Abraham, Isaac and Jacob in the kingdom of heaven'), but the questions which were so pressing for Paul are simply not on the agenda. This is cognate with the fact that Jesus said nothing whatever about circumcision – a point which, as I have argued elsewhere, is a good indication that the early church did not, despite the proposal of the older form-criticism, make up 'words of the Lord' to fit their immediate needs. Circumcision was one of the fiercest controversies in the early church, and the Jesus of the gospels says nothing about it.[4] But it was precisely in that context, the entry of Gentiles into God's people and the question of whether they had to be circumcised or whether they could be full members as they were, that Paul developed his doctrine of justification by faith, to meet (in other words) a situation which, for good reasons, Jesus had not himself faced. It is ironic that some within the 'old perspective' on Paul, by continuing to promote the wrong view of justification as conversion, as the moment of personal salvation and coming to faith rather than God's declaration *about* faith, have reinforced as well a polarization between Jesus and Paul which a more historically grounded and theologically astute reading can and must avoid.

Fourth, what about ethics? There is a well-known aspect of the Jesus/Paul problem which goes like this: granted that Paul occasionally quotes sayings of Jesus (for example, on divorce), and sometimes seems to be alluding to other gospel traditions without actually saying he's doing so, why does he do this so infrequently? If Jesus had taught certain things, why shouldn't Paul have referred to them when they were relevant to his work, as they often were?

The answer is again to do with context, but goes a step further into the question of what Paul thought he was doing (which thus projects us into the middle section of this chapter). We cannot here address the question of which Jesus-traditions Paul may actually have known, and the reason why he may not have known some others. We should not be bullied into accepting the argument that Jesus could not have said anything negative about the Law (as, for instance, in Mark 7) because if he had Paul would not have faced the problem he did in Galatians 2. That is to flatten out two very different situations on the lines I have indicated. In particular, I would respectfully suggest that only someone completely divorced from the real life of actual church communities could suppose that once something definitive had been said by a recognized authority there would from that moment on be no further disputes or puzzles on the subject. But the key thing, which emerges again and again in Paul's writings, is that he wants to teach his churches not just how to behave but *why* to behave like that. Give someone a fish and you feed them for a day; teach someone to fish and you feed them for life. Give someone a hand-me-down ethical maxim and, provided they bow to its authority, they will steer a straight course on that subject alone. Teach someone to think through, from first principles, what it means to live in the new age inaugurated by the death and resurrection of Jesus and in the power of the Spirit, and you equip them not only for that particular topic but for every other question they may meet. That is the kind of thing Paul is doing again and again. Only if we are bent on flattening Jesus and Paul out into 'teachers of religion and ethics', rather than people who believed that God was at last fulfilling his promises and launching his new age upon the world, will we think otherwise.

What I claim to have done in principle, in sketching a portrait of Paul in this book, is to carve out a pathway to a nuanced and satisfying historical integration, complete with full appropriate differentiation, of the respective and very different work of Jesus and of Paul. They were not intending to do the same sort of thing, not because they were at loggerheads but because they were at one in the basic vision which generated their very different vocations. Understanding that unity, and that differentiation, remains a central and vital task of understanding the New Testament and early Christianity.

3. The Work of an Apostle

This brings us to the central section of this chapter: the nature of the work which Paul believed himself called to do. One occasionally hears rumours of great preachers beginning a series on Romans and spending the first three or four weeks on the opening phrases: 'Paul, a servant, called to be an apostle, set apart for the gospel of God'. Most people are eager to get on beyond that to the major themes of the letter, but there is a certain wisdom in focusing on the way in which Paul conceived his own task and what that meant in terms of his agenda for his churches. I shall now attempt to take those opening words of Romans and explain the sense they make within the contexts I sketched in Chapters 2, 3 and 4, and then examine Paul's practice in his churches, growing out of that, in terms of the threefold theology I sketched in Chapters 5, 6 and 7.

a. Servant, apostle, set apart

'Paul, a servant . . .' This is sometimes confusing, because I have argued that, for Paul, Jesus himself was the true and ultimate 'servant of YHWH' spoken of in Isaiah 40—55. That remains the case. But, as various writers have shown compellingly on the basis of careful study of his scriptural echoes and allusions, Paul did indeed believe that he was called now to implement the work of Jesus by himself following a servant-ministry on some aspects at least of the pattern outlined in the Servant Songs. He understands his Gentile ministry in particular to be the implementation of this programme, enabling Israel at last to be a light to the nations. He understands his own sufferings, not as the fulfilment of Isaiah 53 per se, but as part of the servant-programme outlined in the earlier songs. This is to be understood as part of the larger template of Jewish expectation of what it would look like when Israel's destiny was fulfilled and the message of salvation went out to confront the pagan world. 'For your sake we are being killed all day long; we are regarded as sheep to be slaughtered.'[5] Paul's interpretation of his own sufferings for the gospel was that they happened because he and his colleagues were acting out the part of the true Israel, surrounded both by the violent pagans and by renegades from within Israel itself. He saw himself on a map, a grid, constructed as we saw in earlier chapters out of the various controlling narratives of ancient Israel.

'Called to be an apostle': there have been numerous attempts to interpret apostleship in its context, and I do not wish to add to those here, or engage in the debates which they have generated. What I do think we need to take account of is the way in which Paul saw his apostleship in terms of being a *royal emissary*. His apostolic authority, about which we hear a good deal when it is challenged, as in Galatians or 2 Corinthians, is rooted not in himself but in the one who called him and sent him, and in his awareness of a vocation to do a specific, unique and irreplaceable job. He describes it quite cautiously in Romans 15.20: it is his task to name the Messiah where he has not so far been named, rather than building on anyone else's foundation. This may well be directed at an awareness within the small Roman church that its founder had been Peter himself, but whether or not that is so Paul clearly sees himself above all as a *pioneer*. He has the job of going to places which have never heard of Jesus, have never imagined anything so crazy as the story that a young crucified Jew was now the true Lord of the world. I think Paul even glimpsed something of the dark humour of God through which a fanatical right-wing nationalistic Jew should be the one to take to the pagans the news that the Jewish Messiah welcomed them on equal terms – though, to be sure, in one of his most moving reflections on his own apostleship, he sees even this as part of a double task, the second part of which he leaves to God himself to implement, that through his successful work of establishing messianic communities in the Gentile world he is actually making his fellow Jews *jealous*, and so, perhaps, saving some of them.[6] This should, ideally, send us back to 1 Corinthians 9 to reflect more fully on the principles and patterns of his apostolic work, but for that, alas, there is no space here.

'Set apart for God's gospel': the word 'set apart', *aphōrismenos*, has been seen by some as a pun on 'Pharisee', but that remains debatable along with the etymology of the latter word itself. What we can be quite sure of is that Paul mapped out his own vocation, and the implicit narrative within which it made the sense it did, on the grid we described earlier. God's gospel was the good news that the covenant had been fulfilled and that new creation had begun. The great apocalypse had occurred, revealing Jesus as Israel's Messiah. Jesus was therefore Lord of the world, and Caesar was not. This was not just a message which Paul had been given to pass on, like a postman ignorant of the dramatic, life-changing content of the letters he was delivering. It was a message by which his own life was itself defined, shaped and controlled, from the inside as well as on the outside.

b. Redefinitions in practice

We can see what this meant if we look at the three redefinitions of Jewish theology in Chapters 5, 6 and 7 and how they worked out in the actual lives of Paul and his churches. To begin at the beginning, we have noticed how Paul's redefinition of who the one true God actually was came to expression not least in his own variations on Jewish prayers and psalm-like poems. The passage we studied in 1 Corinthians 8.6 is not just part of an argument; it reflects, I believe, Paul's own patterns of prayer, in which he still invoked the one true God in the time-honoured Jewish manner but now did so, with both daring and delight, by including Jesus himself within the very definition of God.

This flowed naturally into his work of building up the church in recognizing, acknowledging and coming to know this God. Though he does not often mention the primary content of his evangelistic preaching, we may be sure that what he says in 1 Thessalonians 1 remained a constant and central theme, as it was in the Areopagus address: to a world full of idols, he declared that there was a living God who had made heaven and earth and who now called all people to account. This involved – and the riot in Ephesus is just one sign of this – regular public confrontation with those for whom idols were big business. This God was powerful; Paul expected to see that power at work within individuals and communities when the gospel was announced. In writing to the Galatians, he takes it for granted that, at the initial preaching of the gospel, powerful deeds – presumably healings – had taken place, and were continuing to take place. These were signs that the true God possessed a power which the other gods did not, a claim no doubt contested by many pagan opponents but insisted on by Paul over and over again.[7] In particular, it was his task to build up the church in the worship and love of the God now made known in Jesus and the Spirit. The life of those who had come to Christian faith was to be rooted in this fresh revelation, which would separate them out drastically from the pagan world around.[8]

More especially, as we saw in Chapter 6, Paul was concerned to build up the church as the reworked chosen people of God. His redefinition of election was first and foremost a matter of hands-on practice, and only then a matter of theory and explanation. Those who were called by God when the gospel was preached were to become a single community, meeting together for worship and prayer, and not least helping one another practically, which would normally include financial support. We should note that that is the normal meaning of *agapē*, love: when he declares to the Thessalonians that he knows they love one another but he wants them to do so more and more, he doesn't mean that he hopes that, as they already have warm fuzzy feelings about one another, those feelings will become yet warmer and fuzzier. He means that as they are already exploring practical ways of supporting one another as though they were part of a single family or business – the normal networks within which such support would take place in the ancient mediterranean world – they should work out in practical terms how to do so more and more.[9] It is interesting that when, writing to the church in Colosse whichhe has not visited, he wants to say that he hears that God has been at work powerfully in their midst, he says that Epaphras, their primary evangelist, has informed him, Paul, about 'their love in the Spirit'.[10] A new community has sprung up in which people from all kinds of backgrounds, with no natural affinity of kin or shared business, are welcoming one another and supporting one another practically. If that isn't God's power at work, Paul indicates, he doesn't know what is.

Paul's practice was therefore to treat the church, and encourage it to regard itself, as God's redeemed humanity, the new model of what it meant to be human. We can see this in obvious and central passages like Romans 12.1–2, where the thrust is as always eschatological: don't be conformed to the present world, but be transformed by the renewal of your minds, so that you may work out in practice what God's will is, what is good and acceptable and perfect. Just as the Qumran sect spoke not infrequently about being the true humanity – to them, declares one passage, all the glory of Adam shall belong, and to their seed for ever – so Paul worked out what it meant to live as God's renewed humanity, and taught his churches what it meant in practice.[11] This is part of the point of his retelling of the story of Abraham in Romans 4, where he consciously reverses the pattern of dehumanization he had sketched earlier.[12] Unlike Adamic humanity, Abraham acknowledged God's power, trusted his promises, grew strong in faith, gave God the glory, and so became fruitful despite apparent impossibility.

The imperative of the gospel meant, above all, unity. We who live with the disunities of the late-modern church can easily forget that church disunity was a fact of life from almost the very beginning – from, at least, the dispute between Hebrews and Hellenists reported in Acts 6. Almost always it had, right from the start, at least an element of ethnic or tribal sympathy at war with the baptismal call to die to old identities and to come alive in and to the new one, the solidarity of the Messiah. Hence Paul's very practical fight to get Jewish Christians and (uncircumcised) Gentile Christians sitting at the same table in Antioch. Indeed, the significance of baptism for him and his work can hardly be overestimated. Just as in some parts of the world today communities such as Hinduism or Islam know very well, often better than many practising Christians, that when someone is baptized they actually change their identity, so for Paul the significance of baptism was that one had come into a new family and had to start behaving as though that was in fact true. Faced with the serious problems that this generated, he didn't back off and say that baptism didn't matter after all. He insisted that it did, urgently, and that the baptized were under great new responsibilities to live as members of the Messiah's body in the power of the Spirit. The consequences of not doing so had to be addressed, not by letting people drift away from the family and its common life but by drawing quite tight boundaries. Some of the things in Paul which we, steeped in late-modern versions of Christianity, find most shocking are his exclusion of impenitent sinners, as in 1 Corinthians 5.

The practice of unity, it seems, means two quite different things. On the one hand, it means that those who take differing views on several subjects – Paul's classic examples are the eating of food offered to idols, or indeed any meat at all, and the keeping or not keeping of holy days – are not to pass judgment on one another. Paul writes in 1 Corinthians 8—10 and Romans 14—15 as one who himself takes the view he characterizes as 'strong': all food is good, God-given, and appropriate if received with thanksgiving. But he knows that if someone else is caused to stumble in their faith by what the 'strong' eat, then the strong are sinning against them, which means against the Messiah himself who died for them. There is thus a delicate balance of mutual respect, maintaining unity across traditional boundaries. But this depends, crucially, on knowing which issues come into this category and which come into that of 1 Corinthians 5 and 6. Incest is not a subject about which there might be two equally valid Christian opinions. Nor is the question of Christians going to law against one another. These are simply ruled out from the start, and those who do them – and a list of other things which Paul throws in here and there – are to be rebuked and reformed or, if they will not come into line, expelled. Paul is sometimes quoted as an exponent of 'tolerance', but that principle, one of the hallmarks of Enlightenment relativism, is both too wide and too shallow. Too wide: there are many things which are not to be tolerated within the church. Paul would not say, of theft, 'Some Christians think that all property is held in common, so they can help themselves to things in other people's houses, while other Christians don't think like that; so let not those who take despise those who don't, and vice versa.' Too shallow: where legitimate differences of opinion occur, Paul does not want Christians to 'tolerate' one another across the divide. He wants them to welcome one another; to rejoice in each other's presence and the rich diversity of God's people; and, ultimately, to worship together with one heart, mind and voice.[13]

The principle of unity lay behind one of Paul's most ambitious hands-on projects, the Collection. It looms large in the Corinthian and Roman letters, both theologically and practically. It is mentioned fleetingly at the end of 1 Corinthians, and far more fully, with more care and labour, in 2 Corinthians 8 and 9 – which contains, in my experience, far and away the hardest Greek in Paul. Then in Romans Paul gives it a particular theological meaning: the Gentiles have shared in the Jews' spiritual privileges, so it is right that the Jews should now share in the Gentiles' material benefits.[14] In other words, the Collection is itself a massive symbol, a great prophetic sign, blazoned across half a continent, trumpeting the fact that the people of God redefined around Jesus the Messiah is a single family and must live as such, by the principle of practical *agapē*. We can only marvel, with boggling minds, at the spectacle of Paul persuading Christians around Greece to part with hard cash on behalf of people they had never met in places they had never visited; at his care to conduct the whole effort with full accountability, not least through accredited representatives of the churches from whom the money had come; at his turning the cash (as presumably he must have done) into a few larger-unit coins rather than carrying huge bags of smaller ones; at his travelling for weeks by land and sea, staying in wayside inns and private homes, with the money always there as both motive and risk; and at his full knowledge that, at the end of the day, the church in Jerusalem might well refuse the gift, since it had come precisely from uncircumcised people, and might well be reckoned to be tainted, to have the smell of idolatry still upon it.[15] This project cannot have been a mere whim, a nice idea dreamed up as a token gesture. Paul must have wanted very, very badly to do it; he must have seen it as a major element in his practical strategy for creating and sustaining the one family of God redefined around the Messiah and in the Spirit. Frustratingly, we do not know the result. But we know what he was trying to do, and why he was trying to do it. That is, perhaps, even more important.

The common life of the body of Christ, as Paul endeavoured to establish and maintain it, was thus bound to appear, on the street, both as a very Jewish thing in the eyes of pagans and as a very pagan thing in the eyes of Jews – which makes it hardly surprising that Paul speaks as he does of the church as a third entity.[16] Within the pagan world there were many clubs, associations, various guilds and groupings of this and that kind. But there were no other groups living as though they were the new version of the human race. Most societies, our own included, dislike (to put it mildly) the apparent arrogance of a claim like that. Many societies, including the ancient Roman world, regarded gatherings of more than a smallish number, for purposes which seemed religious but were nothing to do with the regular civic cult or other recognized deities, as dangerous and subversive. The Jews were well enough known for them to be able to continue their own specific practices and meetings, though they too were of course often regarded as dangerous and subversive – as we can see in the case of the long-established Alexandrian Jewish community, which ran into trouble precisely in our period. So much of what the church was doing and saying must have seemed to the casual pagan onlooker as though it was simply a variety of Judaism, and indeed this verdict was endorsed, greatly to the church's advantage, by Gallio when he was Proconsul in Achaea and gave a key ruling in Corinth.[17] Non-Christian Jews of course resented this deeply, regarding the Christians as heavily compromised on several fronts as well as misguided theologically. In order to understand the practice of Paul's work when living in a city and building up the church, we have to get our minds and imaginations around this complex reality, for which our labels of culture, philosophy, politics, sociology, religion and even theology are all alike inadequate. The many studies of Paul's social world and his location within it have taught us a great deal about not imagining the church in a vacuum. It is vital that we constantly run our theological constructs through this kind of grid so that we can be sure we are understanding what it meant in practice to rethink, and hence rework, the doctrines of monotheism and election.

The practical outworking of Paul's eschatological redefinitions, which we examined in Chapter 7, emerges at several points, notably in the Thessalonian correspondence. Even in the early days of the church in northern Greece, there were clearly some Christians who had taken so seriously Paul's command to 'wait for his son from heaven' that they were giving up all regular work – and then becoming, of course, dependent on other Christians who were still working to supply their daily needs.[18] Paul gives them short shrift. He himself was determined to set an example, even at the cost of the other example he wanted to give, that of labourers deserving their wages.[19]

He worked with his own hands, pursuing his tentmaking calling, in order to make the gospel free of charge. It has sometimes been suggested that part of his motivation in this was to avoid becoming dependent on one particular church, though there were in fact churches, especially his dear friends in northern Greece, who sent him financial help both when he was in prison and when he wasn't. I find it strangely comforting to see Paul negotiating his way through the minefields of church finances and personal resources, and to discover that these minefields were no different in principle from the problems that often beset the church today. Conversely, I wish we could remind ourselves that in all these problems Paul was never being merely pragmatic, but trying at all levels to live out, in severely practical ways, the gospel and theology he was preaching and teaching.

I have given at least a flavour of what Paul's apostolic work looked like in practice, and I have suggested that it should be studied in itself for the way in which it encapsulated the controlling narratives and underlying theology which Paul believed. There is room for a good deal more work on the question of where Paul would have been perceived on the grid of popular imagination and expectation in relation to philosophical movements and teachers, to leaders of political and social pressure groups, and so on. I am particularly interested, though, by the point to which the eye is drawn again and again: that Paul made it his life's work to found and maintain Jew-plus-Gentile churches on Gentile soil within the first Christian generation. There are two ways in which this is significant, which I simply flag up before turning to the last, and brief, section of this chapter and this book.

First, as I have indicated a couple of times, I think Paul believed that Jerusalem was under threat of imminent judgment. The gospel traditions we know from Mark 13 and parallels are well established in early Christianity and echoed at various points by Paul himself.[20] But as Paul reflected on that coming event, as I suggested he was doing in 1 Thessalonians 2.14–16, he must have known as well as anyone what the fallout would be. Jewish non-Christians, and quite likely some Jewish Christians, would at once put the blame on the Christian movement for letting the side down, for undermining Torah-obedience, for fraternizing with pagan idolaters. Gentile Christians, and still more Gentile non-Christians, might well celebrate the overthrow of the nation that had (from their point of view) opposed the gospel from the first. The church would then be split down the middle, along the very seam which Paul spent most of his time stitching up. Indeed, we can see him warding off a possible move down this line in Romans 11. I believe that the note of eschatological urgency which creeps in to Paul here and there arises not least from this, that he knows he has only a generation within which to establish churches whose unity across racial boundaries will be so strong that it will withstand these pressures when they come. The history of the sub-apostolic period indicates both that the pressures were indeed harsh and that the church did in a measure manage to cope; but that is another story.

Second, without wishing to overemphasize the point, we must say once more that the establishment of united communities like this was bound to be seen and felt as a sign within Caesar's world that a new humanity had come into being which challenged, by its very existence as well as by its explicit claims, the claim and rule of Caesar himself. This may be a reason why Paul went west rather than east (a question which is too seldom asked among New Testament scholars, just as is the harder question, why he went through Turkey and Greece rather than along the North African seaboard which shared much of the same culture). I believe he saw the Roman empire, from his perspective of the Old Testament and apocalyptic schematization, as the current great world power; I believe he saw his own Roman citizenship as a paradoxical gift from God to enable him to do this particular work; and I believe he regarded that particular work as being to set up cells loyal to Jesus as Lord across the world where Caesar was lord, raising small but significant flags which heralded the dawn of a different empire, a different *sort* of empire. That, too, is another story.

4. Conclusion: Paul and the Task of the Church

There is space only for a few brief comments on the implications of our picture of Paul for the task of the church in the present day. One word of introduction, and three brief comments.

First, a remark on the principles of hermeneutics as we read Paul. I have outlined in *NTPG* a hermeneutical model, a way of understanding how the Bible is authoritative. It involves understanding the great story, the metanarrative, of the Bible itself, as a five-act play, still unfinished.[21] We do not live in the first act, God's good and unspoiled creation. To think we do would lead to an uncritical acceptance of everything within the world as it is, and hence to a viewpoint shared by virtually no theologian in any tradition. Nevertheless, we do live within the play of which that is indeed the first and irreplaceable act. Nor do we live in the second act, the Fall; to think we do would be to plunge into a dualism, a rejection of the whole created world, which would lead perhaps to some form of Buddhism or Manicheism. Nevertheless, we do live within the play of which that is the second act; certainly Paul would have insisted on this, though many today have wanted to question him, and the larger tradition, at this point. Nor do we live in the third act, the story of Israel BC; to think we do would lead to some kind of odd dispensationalism or 'Jewish Christianity' which would have to ignore, for instance, the letter to the Hebrews, not to mention other large sections of the New Testament. Nevertheless, we do live within the play of which the story of Israel BC is the third act, and to imagine that we don't – as much western Christianity has imagined – is to court theological and practical disasters of which Marcionism and Hitler are simply two of the most obvious examples. Nor do we live in the fourth act: we are not walking around Palestine in the shadow of Jesus of Nazareth as he tells subversive stories, heals cripples, feasts with outcasts, and plans a last dangerous trip to Jerusalem. To suppose that we did – for all that the gospel story possesses a right and proper immediacy and excitement for us – would be to get into several obvious muddles. Nevertheless, the church is constituted precisely as the people for whom the life, ministry, death and resurrection of Jesus are the fourth and decisive act of the play in which we are called to act.

But we do live in the fifth act. This act begins at Easter; its opening scenes include Pentecost; part of its early task was so to tell and write the story of Jesus, so to guide and direct the tiny church by the written as well as the spoken word, as to form basic and non-negotiable parameters for how we today, the church still in the fifth act albeit several scenes later, are to improvise our way from where this act began to where it is supposed to end.

This fifth act, in which the church is called to live and work, is therefore characterized by two things. First, it has firm and fixed foundations, including a definite closing scene which is already sketched in Romans 8, 1 Corinthians 15, Ephesians 1, Colossians 1 and Revelation 21 and 22. Second, it has the command, under the Spirit, *to improvise a way through the unscripted period between the opening scenes and the closing one.* Note: no musician would ever suppose that improvising means playing out of tune or time. On the contrary, it means knowing extremely well where one is in the implicit structure, and listening intently to the other players so that what we all do together, however spontaneously, makes sense as a whole.

That is the kind of hermeneutic I envisage as I read, and preach from, Paul's letters today. What he wrote is part of the non-negotiable foundation of the act we are living in. The earlier changes of act, particularly the shift away from act 3 to act 4 and then to act 5, necessarily involve particular hermeneutical moves in which, for instance, circumcision and animal sacrifice, once strictly mandatory, have now become irrelevant. That is what was at stake in such debates as those in the second chapter of Galatians and the fifteenth chapter of the Acts of the Apostles. But no such hermeneutical shift separates us from Paul. We are part of the same single movement of the Spirit, and must regard his letters, like the rest of the New Testament, as 'our book' in a way which is not true of, say, Leviticus or even Isaiah.

Having said that, it is of course urgent and vital that we explore, in that improvisatory fashion, the ways in which, within our own very different culture, we can rightly reappropriate his gospel in the world of late modernity, postmodernity, post-colonialism, neo-imperialism, and all the other things that swirl around our heads at the start of the twenty-first century. I believe it is part of the task of the church today to accept the postmodern critique of modernity but to insist that it is not the last word. Modernity stands accused of arrogance, with its technology, its philosophy, its economics and its empires – and, in a measure at least, its theology and exegesis. Postmodernity, with Marx, Freud and Nietzsche in its vanguard, has made its point. The world of the Enlightenment had a lot to do with money, sex and power. But, despite the misplaced enthusiasm of some, postmodernity does not give us a new home, a place to stay. What it provides is a fresh statement of the doctrine of the Fall, which in Christian theology ought always to invite a fresh statement, in symbol and practice as well as word, of redemption. I believe that part of the task of the church in our own day is to pioneer a way through postmodernity and out the other side, not back to modernity in its various, even in its Christian, guises, but into a new world, a new culture, which nobody else is shaping and which we have a chance to. Paul has a vital role to play in that task. I briefly mention three aspects of this.[22]

First, the reconstruction of the self. Modernity's all-important Self, proud, self-reliant, knowable and self-affirming, has been deconstructed into a mass of floating signifiers. Having mentioned improvisation a moment ago, let me quote from the jazz musician Charlie Mingus: 'When I play, I'm trying to play the truth of who I am. The problem is that I'm changing all the time.' Welcome to postmodernity, where even the 'I' at the centre, Descartes's last bastion, turns out to be an unreliable kaleidoscopic mirror. But with Paul there is a way through, not to a reconstruction of an arrogant modernist Self, but to a new way of being human, a way that is rooted, through baptism, in the Messiah, or more particularly in the love of the one God revealed in him. If anyone is in Christ – new creation! Not 'Cogito, ergo sum' but 'Amor, ergo sum': I am loved, therefore I am. That is where Paul is in Galatians, 1 Corinthians and above all Romans.[23]

Second, the reconstruction of knowing. Modernity claimed to be able to know things objectively. Postmodernity has shown up the claim as a power-play. But with Paul, as with much Christian thinking, the basic Christian mode of knowing is love. In love, the person who is loving is simultaneously affirming the Otherness of that which is loved and their own deep involvement with that Other. This takes us way beyond the objective/subjective divide (and the spurious reduction of everything to currency and commodity) and into an epistemological world which could have incalculable effects for how we begin to live in this new century. Not only justification by faith but that knowing of God, the world and one another for which Paul strived will see us go forward intellectually and culturally.

Third, the reconstruction of the great story. The grand narrative of modernity, of progress and Enlightenment, has run out of steam in most areas, though still not, alas, in western imperialism. With it, all grand narratives have been seen as exploitative, as power-plays, as attempts to snatch the high ground and rule other stories out of consideration. But, once more, the story which Paul tells, and equally importantly the story he lived out day by day, is a story not of power but of love. There is, of course, a power which comes with that, but it is made perfect only in weakness. The paradox of the cross is the great theme of the new grand story, preventing it ever – if it is true to itself – from being twisted by knaves to make a trap for fools. When faced precisely with a challenge to his apostleship and consequent authority in 2 Corinthians and Galatians, Paul reaches down to the depths of the Christian retelling of the Jewish story in order to say again, and to live again, the message which could create a fresh sense of human flourishing, nourished by a fresh appropriation of the Christian gospel, in our own day. 'God forbid that I should glory,' he writes, 'except in the cross of the Messiah, by which the world is crucified to me and I to the world. Neither circumcision nor uncircumcision matters, but only new creation.' 'Jesus is Lord, and at his name every knee shall bow.' 'The whole creation shall be set free from its bondage to decay and share the freedom of the glory of God's children.' 'God will be all in all.'[24] That is the story. That is the foundation of all knowledge. That is the rock on which Paul invites us to stand as ourselves new creatures, called, justified and glorified, from which we go to the dangerous and exhilarating task of being, knowing and telling. The question of Pauline hermeneutics in the twenty-first century may well turn out to be a matter not so much of comprehension, but of courage.

Notes

Preface

1 These three books are abbreviated hereafter as *What St Paul*, *Climax* and *Romans* respectively. I shall make reference, too, to the three volumes of my series 'Christian Origins and the Question of God', namely *The New Testament and the People of God* (*NTPG*), *Jesus and the Victory of God* (*JVG*) and *The Resurrection of the Son of God* (*RSG*) (SPCK and Fortress Press: 1992, 1996 and 2003 respectively).

1 Paul's World, Paul's Legacy

1 2 Cor. 10.5.
2 Cf. *NTPG*, Part II.
3 See particularly B. W. Longenecker (ed.), *Narrative Dynamics in Paul: A Critical Assessment* (Louisville and London: Westminster John Knox Press, 2002).
4 R. B. Hays, *The Faith of Jesus Christ: The Narrative Substructure of Galatians 3:1—4:11*, 2nd edn (Grand Rapids and Cambridge: Eerdmans; Dearborn, Mich.: Dove Booksellers, 2002 [1983]).
5 E. P. Sanders, *Paul and Palestinian Judaism* (London: SCM Press, 1977), is normally regarded as the foundation text of the 'new perspective'.
6 E. Champlin, *Nero* (Cambridge, Mass.: Harvard University Press, 2003), here at 237.
7 R. Kipling, 'When Earth's Last Picture is Painted', in *Rudyard Kipling's Verse: Inclusive Edition, 1885–1926* (London: Hodder & Stoughton, 1927), 223f.
8 E. Käsemann, *Commentary on Romans*, ET of 3rd edn (Grand Rapids and London: Eerdmans and SCM Press, 1980 [1973]), viii.
9 R. Morgan, *The Nature of New Testament Theology* (London: SCM Press, 1973), 44.

2 Creation and Covenant

1 *NTPG*, 260–8.
2 Isa. 51.12–16.
3 E. P. Sanders, *Paul and Palestinian Judaism* (London: SCM Press, 1977), 81–107, 236–8, and esp. 420f.
4 See *Climax*, ch. 5 for full details.

5 For details, see *RSG*, ch. 7.
6 Note the summing up in v. 56: the sting of death is sin, and the power of sin is the law.
7 For full details, see *Romans*.
8 On this see esp. *Romans*, 658–66.
9 S. Westerholm, *Perspectives Old and New on Paul: The 'Lutheran' Paul and his Critics* (Grand Rapids, Mich.: Eerdmans, 2004) is the most recent example of this false either/or, repeated over and over throughout the book, e.g. 257f.

3 Messiah and Apocalyptic

1 1 Cor. 2.1–2.
2 See *Climax*, chs. 2 and 3.
3 For details, see e.g. *NTPG*, 307–20; *JVG*, 481–6.
4 Further details in *Climax*, chs. 2 and 3.
5 1 Cor. 3.16f.; 6.19.
6 *Climax*, 46f., drawing on the work of my doctoral dissertation of 1980; the reference is to 2 Sam. 20.1; 1 Kings 12.16.
7 Gal. 4.4; Rom. 8.3; 8.32.
8 Ps. 72.8.
9 K. Koch, *The Rediscovery of Apocalyptic*, ET (London: SCM Press, 1972 [1970]).
10 J. C. Beker, *Paul the Apostle: The Triumph of God in Life and Thought* (Philadelphia: Fortress Press, 1980); J. L. Martyn, *Galatians: A New Translation with Introduction and Commentary* (New York: Doubleday, 1997).
11 In e.g. *NTPG*, ch. 10.
12 This twofold created order is better not described as a 'dualism', because part of the point of it is normally that heaven and earth are two parts of the same good (though fallen) creation, not that heaven is the good bit and earth the bad bit. I prefer the term 'duality' to indicate a two-sided reality in which the two sides, both parts of God's good creation, exist in a complex but coherent relationship. On all this, see *NTPG*, 297–9.

4 Gospel and Empire

1 Graham Robb, *Strangers: Homosexual Love in the Nineteenth Century* (London: Picador, 2003).
2 Cf. E. R. Goodenough, *The Politics of Philo Judaeus: Practice and Theory* (Hildesheim: Georg Olms, 1967); E. Champlin, *Nero* (Cambridge, Mass.: Harvard University Press, 2003).
3 Richard Hays, *Echoes of Scripture in the Letters of Paul* (New Haven: Yale University Press, 1989).

4 Hays, *Echoes*, 29–32.
5 I and others have set all this out at much greater length: cf. e.g. the three books edited by R. Horsley, *Paul and Empire* (1997), *Paul and Politics* (2000), and *Paul and the Roman Imperial Order* (2004), all published by Trinity Press International (Harrisburg, Pa.), and my article 'A Fresh Perspective on Paul?', *Bulletin of the John Rylands Library* 83, no. 1 (2001), 21–39.
6 1 Sam. 8.10–18.
7 Amos 1.3—2.8; Isa. 10.5–19.
8 E.g. Isa. 13.
9 Jer. 50—51.
10 Dan. 7.
11 Dan. 3.30; 6.28; Jer. 29.1–9.
12 We might note at this point the comparative scarcity of the title 'saviour' in the New Testament; and we might note, as a pointer to further work that needs doing here, its frequency in the Pastorals: 2 Tim. 1.10; Titus 2.13, etc.
13 For the following point I draw on my article 'Paul's Gospel and Caesar's Empire' in Horsley (ed.), *Paul and Politics*, 160–83.
14 P. Oakes, *Philippians: From People to Letter* (Cambridge: Cambridge University Press, 2001).
15 Another passage where Paul does the same is Rom. 10.12f.
16 B. Winter, *Seek the Welfare of the City: Christians as Benefactors and Citizens* (Grand Rapids and Carlisle: Eerdmans and Paternoster Press, 1994), 134–42, following a much earlier suggestion by W. Lütgert.
17 Acts 18.12–17.
18 Eph. 6.10–20; 1 Cor. 15.25–28; 1 Thess. 5.8.
19 Rom. 1.3f.; 15.12.
20 On the competence of 'ordinary' people to pick up coded references, I refer once again to Champlin, *Nero*.

5 Rethinking God

1 Cf. *NTPG*, ch. 9.
2 This book was substantially written before Francis Watson published his remarkable book *Paul and the Hermeneutics of Faith* (London: T. & T. Clark International, 2004), but at this point I am in obvious, if implicit, dialogue with him.
3 On 'kingdom of God' in this period cf. *JVG*, 202–26.
4 Rom. 10.4.
5 A brilliant fresh exploration of relevant themes is found in the new book by Larry Hurtado, *Lord Jesus Christ: Devotion to Jesus in Earliest Christianity* (Grand Rapids, Mich.: Eerdmans, 2003). My own former

writings on this subject, to which the present section is indebted, include *Climax*, Part II and *What St Paul*, ch. 4.

6 For what follows cf. *Romans* 658–66 and below, 125.
7 Rom. 10.12, quoting Joel 2.32.
8 See *Romans* 629–31.
9 See *Climax*, ch. 4.
10 More details in *Climax*, ch. 6.
11 1 Cor. 8.4.
12 Deut. 6.4.
13 See *JVG*, ch. 13.
14 Rom. 4.24f.
15 On the Holy Spirit in Paul, see esp. G. D. Fee, *God's Empowering Presence: The Holy Spirit in the Letters of Paul* (Peabody, Mass.: Hendrickson, 1994).
16 At this point I am particularly indebted to Sylvia C. Keesmaat, *Paul and His Story: (Re)Interpreting the Exodus Tradition* (Sheffield: Sheffield Academic Press, 1999).
17 Cf. 2 Cor. 2.22; 5.5; Eph. 1.14.
18 See further *Romans* 577–81. This is at the heart of my response to Watson, *Paul and the Hermeneutics of Faith*, on the subject of whether Paul envisaged some kind of 'doing of the Torah' through Christian faith.
19 Above, 98.
20 W. Meeks, *The First Urban Christians: The Social World of the Apostle Paul* (New Haven: Yale University Press, 1983), ch. 6.

6 Reworking God's People

1 D. A. Carson, P. T. O'Brien and M. A. Seifrid (eds.), *Justification and Variegated Nomism*, 2 vols. (Tübingen and Grand Rapids: Mohr Sieback and Baker Academic, 2001, 2004).
2 Throughout this chapter I am in implicit dialogue with, among others, D. Harink, *Paul among the Postliberals: Pauline Theology Beyond Christendom and Modernity* (Grand Rapids, Mich.: Brazos Press, 2003), ch. 4.
3 Cf. Rom. 4.11, where 'sign of *dikaiosynē*' is Paul's explanatory summary of Gen. 17.11, 'sign of *diathēkē* [covenant]'.
4 See *Climax*, ch. 7.
5 E.g. P. Tomson, *Paul and the Jewish Law: Halakha in the Letters of the Apostle to the Gentiles* (Assen/Maastricht and Minneapolis: Van Gorcom and Fortress Press, 1990); M. Bockmuehl, *Jewish Law in Gentile Churches: Halakhah and the Beginning of Christian Public Ethics* (Edinburgh: T. and T. Clark, 2000).
6 E.g. K. Stendahl, *Final Account: Paul's Letter to the Romans* (Minneapolis: Fortress Press, 1995).

7 This is the point never grasped by a long line of writers of whom Harink, *Paul among the Postliberals*, ch. 4, is simply the most recent.
8 Rom. 13.12–14; Phil. 2.12–16; Eph. 5.11–14; 1 Thess. 5.4–6.

7 Reimagining God's Future

1 Isa. 55.13.
2 Dan. 7.
3 Amos 5.18.
4 Mal. 3.1–4.
5 Hag. 2.21–23.
6 See esp. *NTPG*, ch. 10; *JVG*, *passim*; cf. too 'In Grateful Dialogue' in C. C. Newman (ed.), *Jesus and the Restoration of Israel* (Downers Grove, Ill. and Carlisle: InterVarsity Press and Paternoster Press, 1999), 257–61.
7 Ezra 9.7; Neh. 9.36f.
8 Jer. 25.12; cf. Ezra 1.1.
9 Dan. 9.24.
10 Josephus, *Jewish War* 6.312–15.
11 See esp. *JVG*, ch. 13.
12 Zech. 14.9.
13 Rom. 2.16; 2 Cor. 5.10.
14 Phil. 2.10f.; 1 Cor. 15.24–28.
15 E.g. Rom. 4.24f.; 6.4.
16 *RSG*, *passim*, esp. Part II.
17 Not that Jesus only became Messiah at his resurrection; for Paul, his death is already messianic, as in 1 Cor. 1.23 or 15.3; rather, the resurrection declared that status to the world, as in Rom. 1.4.
18 Cf. Rom. 5.12–14; 7.9. I am grateful to Prof. John Barclay for stressing this point to me in conversation.
19 Full details in *Climax*, ch. 7.
20 The first novel in the series was entitled *Left Behind: A Novel of the Earth's Last Days* (Carol Stream, Ill.: Tyndale House Publishers, 1996). There are now 12 books in the series, plus a children's version, DVDs, a 'Left Behind Trivia Game', and sundry other spin-offs.
21 See too ch. 3 above.
22 Both of these can also be seen in the word *epiphaneia*, 'manifestation', which occurs mostly in the Pastorals (1 Tim. 6.14; 2 Tim. 1.10; 4.1; 8; Titus 2.13; correlated with *sōtēr* in Titus 2.13, 2 Tim. 1.10) and which suggests, to me at least, a far more politically confrontative mood there than is normally recognized.
23 Rom. 8.34.
24 Phil. 3.20.
25 1 Cor. 6.3.

26 See esp. *RSG*, ch. 6.
27 2 Cor. 1.22; 5.5.
28 Rom. 8.23; Eph. 1.14.
29 Rom. 2.25–29; 7.4–6; and – an often-neglected passage on this theme – Rom. 8.4–8.
30 Gal. 1.4; 5.18.
31 Gal. 5.23.
32 Phil. 1.19; cf., e.g. 1 Thess. 1.6.
33 1 Cor. 12.3; Eph. 2.8.
34 Rom. 8.11.
35 Phil. 4.1; cf. 2.16; 1 Thess. 2.19; 3.9. I am grateful to Dr Lionel North for his stress on this point in a seminar paper in Cambridge some years ago.
36 Rom. 5.5; 8.28.
37 Rom. 8.18–25.
38 Rom. 8.17f., 28–30.
39 Rom. 8.26f.
40 Rom. 2.16; 2.1–5; 2.25–29; 8.1–11.
41 Rom. 14.5–12; Phil. 2.10f.; 3.20f.
42 1 Cor. 15.20–28; 1 Thess. 4.13—5.11.
43 Cf. Eph. 4.17–24.
44 Rom. 8.12–17.
45 1 Cor. 4.9.
46 1 Cor. 5.1–5; 2 Cor. 13.1–10.
47 Col. 1.23.
48 1 Thess. 2.10–12; 3.1–13.

8 Jesus, Paul and the Task of the Church

1 For a previous discussion of this theme, cf. *What St Paul*, ch. 10.
2 Luke 18.14.
3 Gen. 38.26.
4 Cf. *NTPG*, 421; *JVG*, 373, 381f.
5 Rom. 8.36, quoting Ps. 44.22 (LXX 43.23).
6 Rom. 11.15.
7 Rom. 1.18–23; 1 Cor. 12.2; Eph 1.19–23; etc.
8 Gal. 4.8–11.
9 1 Thess. 4.9–12.
10 Col. 1.9.
11 4QPs37 3.1f.
12 Cf. Rom. 4.18–22 with 1.18–32; cf. *Romans*, 500.
13 Cf. esp. Rom. 15.7–13.
14 Rom. 15.27.
15 Cf. Rom. 15.31.

16 1 Cor. 10.32 ('Jews, Greeks and the church of God').
17 Acts 18.12–17; cf. 75f. above.
18 1 Thess. 1.10; 4.11f.; 2 Thess. 3.6–13.
19 1 Cor. 9.12–18; and the references in the previous note.
20 E.g. 1 Thess. 5.2 with Matt. 24.43; Luke 17.24.
21 Cf. *NTPG*, ch. 5; and *Scripture and the Authority of God* (London: SPCK, 2005; in the USA *The Last Word* [San Francisco CA: Harper San Francisco, 2005]), ch. 10, with which the present section corresponds rather closely.
22 For fuller exploration of these themes, cf. *The Myth of the Millennium* (in USA: *The Millennium Myth*) (London and Louisville: SPCK and Westminster John Knox Press, 1999), ch. 3; also *The Challenge of Jesus* (London and Downers Grove, Ill.: SPCK and InterVarsity Press, 2000), ch. 8.
23 E.g. Gal. 2.20; 4.9; 1 Cor. 8.3; Rom. 5.5–11; 8.31–39.
24 Gal. 6.14f.; Phil. 2.10f.; Rom. 8.21; 1 Cor. 15.28.

Bibliography

Beker, J. Christiaan. *Paul the Apostle*. Edinburgh: T. & T. Clark, 1980.

Bockmuehl, Marcus. *Jewish Law in Gentile Churches: Halakhah and the Beginning of Christian Public Ethics*. Edinburgh: T. & T. Clark, 2000.

Bultmann, Rudolf. *Theology of the New Testament*. London: SCM Press, 1952–55.

Carson, D. A., P. T. O'Brien and M. A. Seifrid (eds.). *Justification and Variegated Nomism*, 2 vols. Tübingen/Grand Rapids: Mohr Siebeck/Baker, 2001, 2004.

Casey, P. M. 'Monotheism, Worship, and Christological Developments in the Pauline Churches.' Pages 214–33 in *The Jewish Roots of Christological Monotheism*, ed. C. C. Newman, J. R. Davila and G. S. Lewis. Leiden: Brill, 1999.

Champlin, Edward. *Nero*. Cambridge, Mass.: Belknap, 2003.

Collins, John J. *The Apocalyptic Imagination: An Introduction to the Jewish Matrix of Christianity*. New York: Crossroad, 1984.

Davies, W. D. *Paul and Rabbinic Judaism: Some Rabbinic Elements in Pauline Theology*, 4th edn. Philadelphia: Fortress Press, 1980.

Dunn, James D. G. *Jesus, Paul and the Law: Studies in Mark and Galatians*. London/Louisville: SPCK/Westminster John Knox Press, 1990.

—. *The Theology of Paul the Apostle*. Grand Rapids: Eerdmans, 1998.

Engberg-Pedersen, Troels. *Paul and the Stoics*. Louisville: Westminster John Knox Press, 2000.

Fee, Gordon. *God's Empowering Presence: The Holy Spirit in the Letters of Paul*. Peabody: Hendrickson, 1994.

Haacker, K. *The Theology of Romans*. Cambridge: Cambridge University Press, 2003.

Hays, Richard B. *Echoes of Scripture in the Letters of Paul*. New Haven: Yale University Press, 1989.

—. *The Faith of Jesus Christ: The Narrative Substructure of Galatians 3:1–4:11*, 2nd edn. Grand Rapids: Eerdmans, 2002.

Horsley, Richard (ed.). *Paul and Empire: Religion and Power in Roman Imperial Society*. Harrisburg, PA.: Trinity Press International, 1997.

—. *Paul and Politics: Ekklesia, Israel, Imperium, Interpretation*. Harrisburg, PA.: Trinity Press International, 2000.

—. *Paul and the Roman Imperial Order*. Harrisburg, PA.: Trinity Press International, 2004.

Hurtado, Larry. *Lord Jesus Christ: Devotion to Jesus in Earliest Christianity*. Grand Rapids: Eerdmans, 2003.

Käsemann, Ernst. *Commentary on Romans*. Grand Rapids: Eerdmans, 1980.

Keesmaat, Sylvia C. *Paul and His Story: (Re)interpreting the Exodus Tradition*. *Journal for the Study of the New Testament* Supplement Series 181. Sheffield: Sheffield Academic Press, 1999.

Kim, S. *The Origin of Paul's Gospel*, 2nd edn. Tübingen: Mohr Siebeck, 2002.

Koch, Klaus. *The Rediscovery of Apocalyptic*. London: SCM Press, 1972.

LaHaye, Timothy F. and Jerry B. Jenkins. *Left Behind: A Novel of the Earth's Last Days*. Carol Stream, IL.: Tyndale House, 1996.

Longenecker, Bruce W. (ed.). *Narrative Dynamics in Paul: A Critical Assessment*. Louisville/London: Westminster John Knox Press, 2002.

Marcus, Joel and M. L. Soards (eds.). *Apocalyptic and the New Testament: Essays in Honor of J. Louis Martyn*. *Journal for the Study of the New Testament* Supplement Series 24. Sheffield: Sheffield Academic Press, 1989.

Martyn, J. Louis. *Theological Issues in the Letters of Paul*. Nashville: Abingdon Press, 1997.

Meeks, Wayne A. *The First Urban Christians: The Social World of the Apostle Paul*. New Haven: Yale University Press, 2003.

Morgan, Robert (ed.). *The Nature of New Testament Theology: The Contribution of William Wrede and Adolf Schlatter*. London: SCM Press, 1973.

Nanos, Mark. *The Mystery of Romans: The Jewish Context of Paul's Letter*. Minneapolis: Fortress Press, 1996.

Oakes, Peter. *Philippians: From People to Letter*. Cambridge: Cambridge University Press, 2001.

Ridderbos, Herman. *Paul: An Outline of His Theology*. Grand Rapids: Eerdmans, 1997.

Robb, Graham. *Strangers: Homosexual Love in the Nineteenth Century*. London: Picador, 2003.

Roetzel, Calvin J. *Paul a Jew on the Margins*. Louisville: Westminster John Knox Press, 2003.

Rowland, Christopher. *The Open Heaven: A Study of Apocalyptic in Judaism and Early Christianity*. London: SPCK, 1982.

Sanders, E. P. *Paul and Palestinian Judaism: A Comparison of Patterns of Religion*. London: SCM Press, 1977.

Stendahl, Krister. *Paul Among Jews and Gentiles and Other Essays*. Philadelphia: Fortress Press, 1976.

Tacitus, Cornelius. *Agricola, Germania, Dialogue on Oratory*, tr. M. Hutton *et al.*, 2nd edn, Loeb Classical Library. Cambridge, Mass.: Harvard University Press, 1970 [1914].

Tomson, Peter J. *Paul and the Jewish Law: Halakha in the Letters of the Apostle to the Gentiles*. Assen: Van Gorcum, 1990.

Watson, Francis. *Paul and the Hermeneutics of Faith*. Edinburgh: T. & T. Clark, 2004.

Westerholm, Stephen. *Perspectives Old and New on Paul.* Grand Rapids: Eerdmans, 2003.

Whiteley, D. E. H. *The Theology of St Paul.* Oxford: Blackwell, 1964.

Winter, Bruce. *Seek the Welfare of the City: Christians as Benefactors and Citizens.* Grand Rapids, PA./Carlisle: Eerdmans/Paternoster Press, 1994.

Winter, Bruce and Andrew D. Clarke (eds.). *The Book of Acts in its Ancient Literary Setting.* Grand Rapids, PA./Carlisle: Eerdmans/Paternoster Press, 1993.

Witherington, Ben III. *The Paul Quest: The Renewed Search for the Jew of Tarsus.* Downers Grove, IL.: InterVarsity Press, 1998.

Wright, N. T. *The Climax of the Covenant: Christ and the Law in Pauline Theology.* Edinburgh: T. & T. Clark, 1991.

—. *Jesus and the Victory of God.* Christian Origins and the Question of God 2. London/Minneapolis: SPCK/Fortress Press, 1996.

__. *The Myth of the Millennium.* London: SPCK, 1999. (In USA as *The Millennium Myth.* Louisville: Westminster John Knox Press, 1999.)

__. *The New Testament and the People of God.* Christian Origins and the Question of God 1. London/Minneapolis: SPCK/Fortress Press, 1992.

—. *The Resurrection of the Son of God.* Christian Origins and the Question of God 3. London/Minneapolis: SPCK/Fortress Press, 2003.

—. *Romans.* New Interpreters Bible 10. Nashville: Abingdon Press, 2002.

__. *Scripture and the Authority of God.* London/San Francisco: SPCK/HarperSanFrancisco, 2005.

—. *What St Paul Really Said.* Oxford/Grand Rapids: Lion/Eerdmans, 1997.

Index of Selected Topics

Index of Modern Authors

Index of Text References

Old Testament

New Testament

Apocrypha and Pseudepigrapha

Dead Sea Scrolls